EASY PIANO

Disney MARY POPPINS RETURNS
MUSIC FROM THE MOTION PICTURE SOUNDTRACK

T0068389

Disney

MARY POPPINS RETURNS

Motion Picture Artwork TM & Copyright © 2018 Disney

ISBN 978-1-5400-4467-9

HAL•LEONARD®

Visit Hal Leonard Online at
www.halleonard.com

Contact us:
Hal Leonard
7777 West Bluemound Road
Milwaukee, WI 53213
Email: info@halleonard.com

In Europe, contact:
Hal Leonard Europe Limited
42 Wigmore Street
Marylebone, London, W1U 2RN
Email: info@halleonardeurope.com

In Australia, contact:
Hal Leonard Australia Pty. Ltd.
4 Lentara Court
Cheltenham, Victoria, 3192 Australia
Email: info@halleonard.com.au

(Underneath the)
LOVELY LONDON SKY

Music by MARC SHAIMAN
Lyrics by SCOTT WITTMAN and MARC SHAIMAN

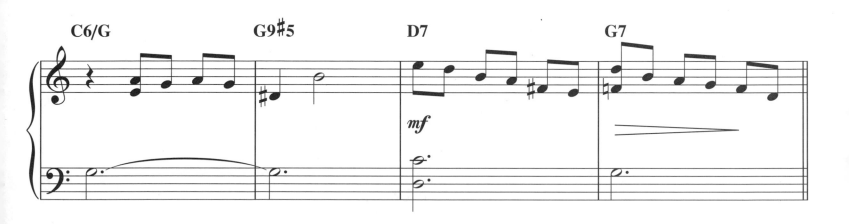

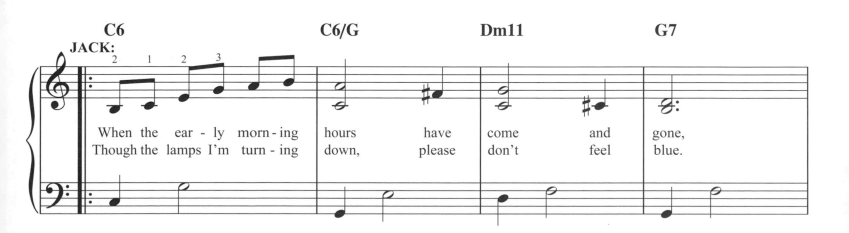

10

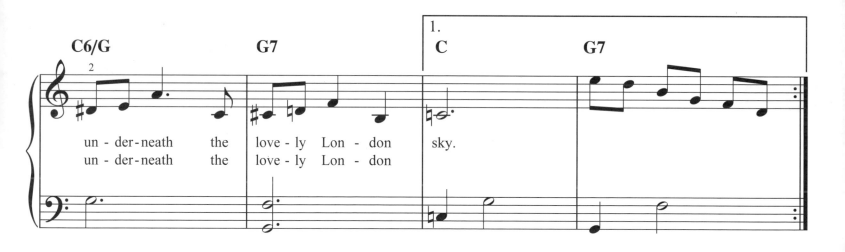

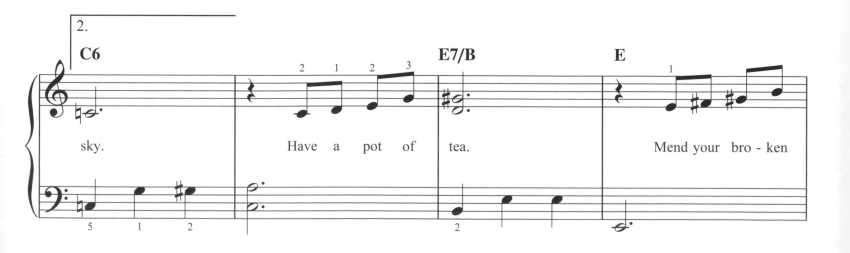

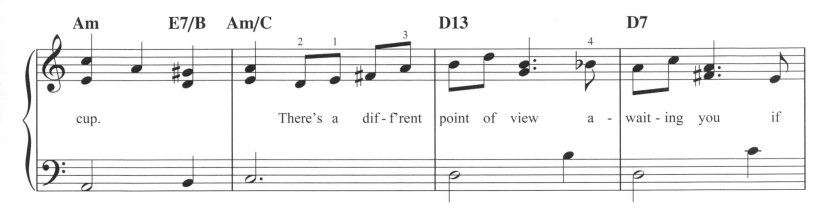

Am   E7/B   Am/C   D13   D7

cup.   There's a dif-f'rent point of view a - wait-ing you if

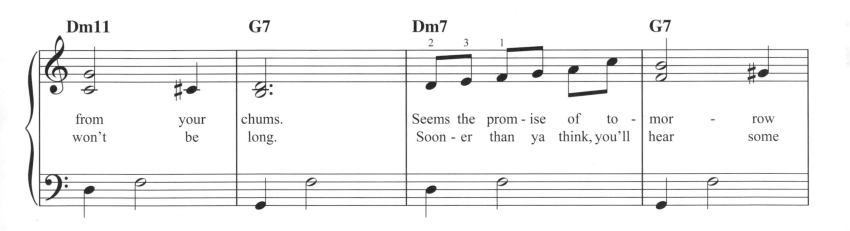

Dm7   G13   N.C.   C6   C6/G

you would just look up! I know yes - ter - day, you had to bor - row
                              soon this slump-'ll dis-ap-pear;   it

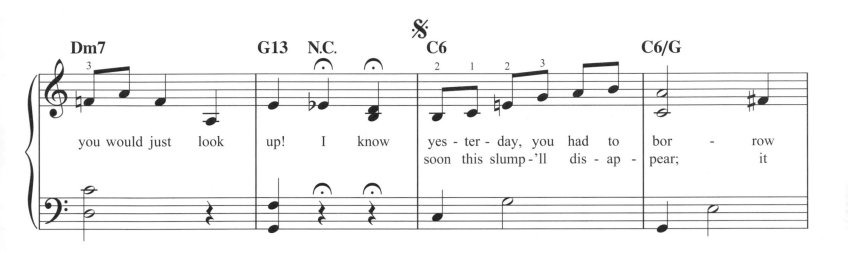

Dm11   G7   Dm7   G7

from   your   chums.   Seems the prom-ise of to - mor - row
won't   be   long.   Soon - er than ya think, you'll hear some

C6   C6/G   C6   E+

nev - er   comes.   But, since you dreamed the night a - way, _____ to-
bright new   song.   So, hold on tight to those you love, _____ and

12

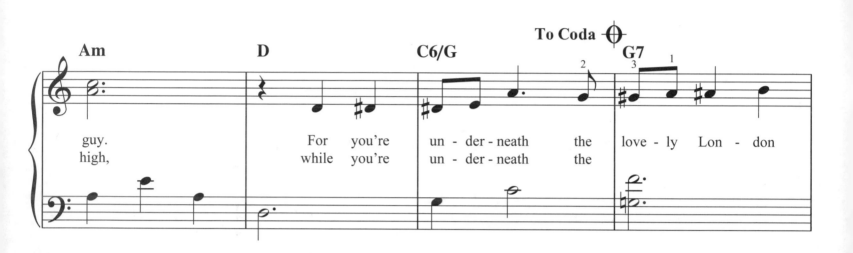

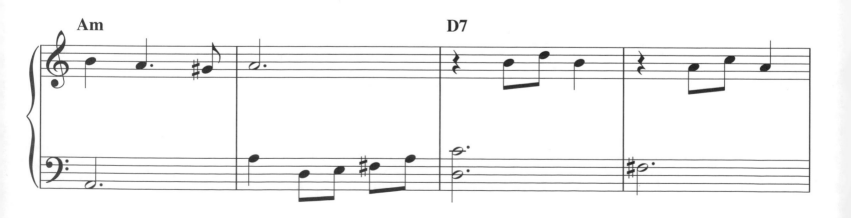

Dm7   G7   D.S. al Coda

Lis - ten:

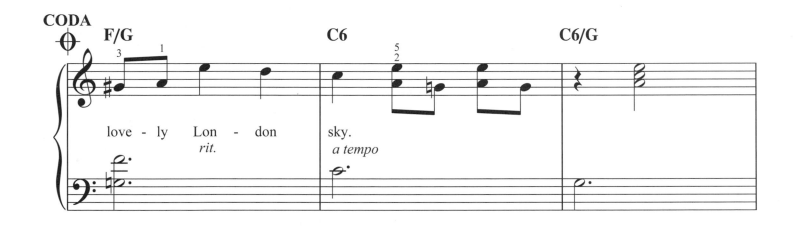

CODA

F/G   C6   C6/G

love - ly Lon - don
rit.

sky.
a tempo

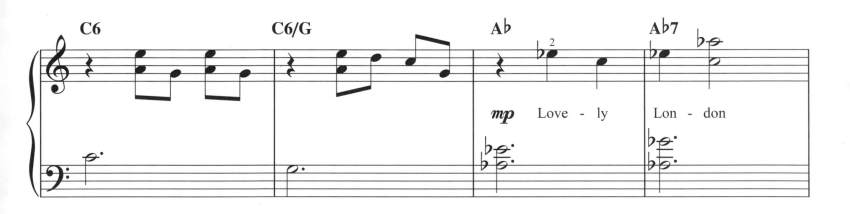

C6   C6/G   Ab   Ab7

mp Love - ly   Lon - don

C6

sky.

p

A CONVERSATION

Music by MARC SHAIMAN
Lyrics by SCOTT WITTMAN and MARC SHAIMAN

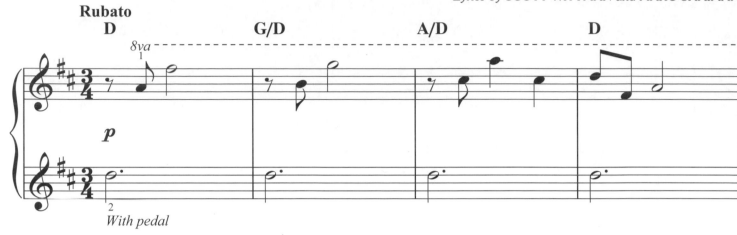

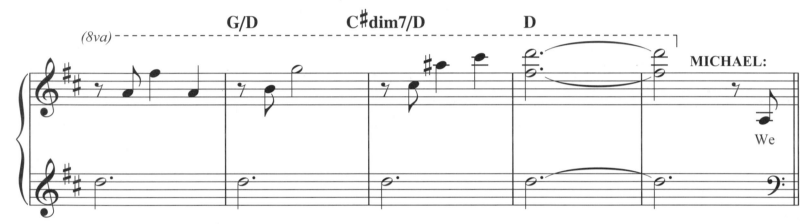

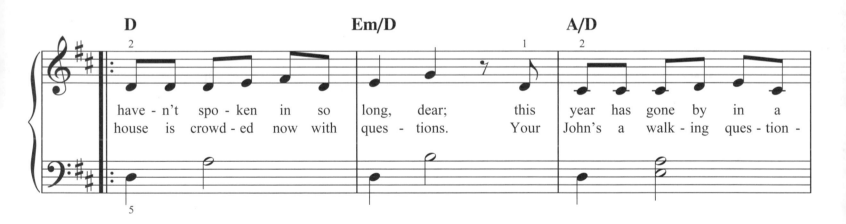

have-n't spo-ken in so long, dear; this year has gone by in a
house is crowd-ed now with ques-tions. Your John's a walk-ing ques-tion-

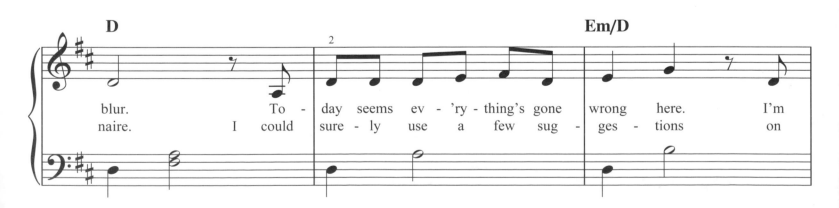

blur. To - day seems ev-'ry-thing's gone wrong here. I'm
naire. I could sure-ly use a few sug - ges - tions on

looking for the way things were. I
how to brush our daughter's hair. When

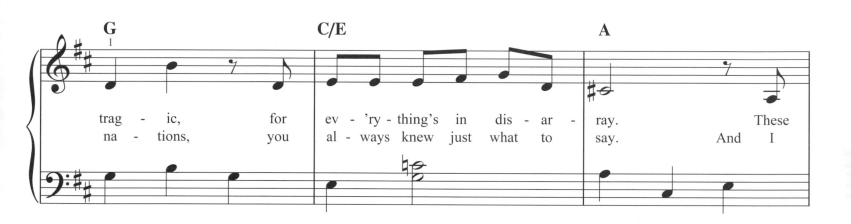

know you'd laugh and call me tragic, for
Georgie needed expla- nations, you

ev-'ry-thing's in dis-ar- ray. These
al-ways knew just what to say. And I

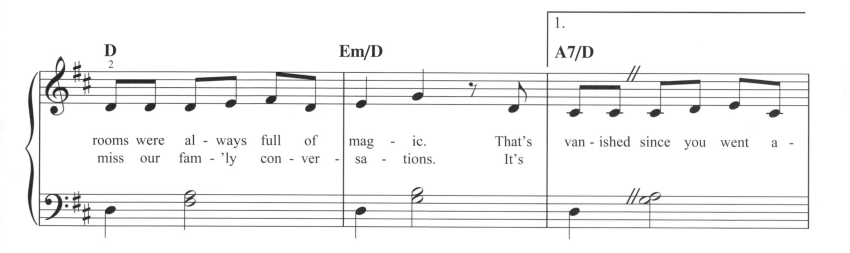

rooms were al-ways full of magic. That's
miss our fam-'ly con-ver- sa- tions. It's

vanished since you went a-

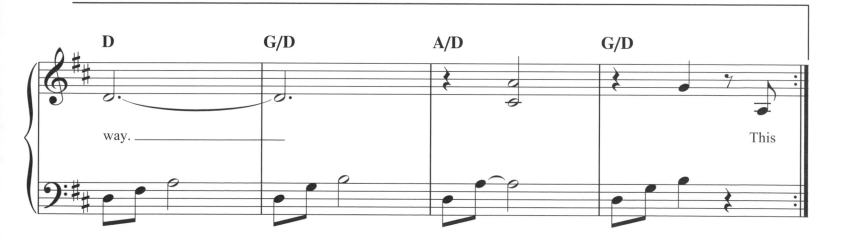

way.

This

2. Slower

Tempo I

si - lent since you went a - way.   Win - ter has

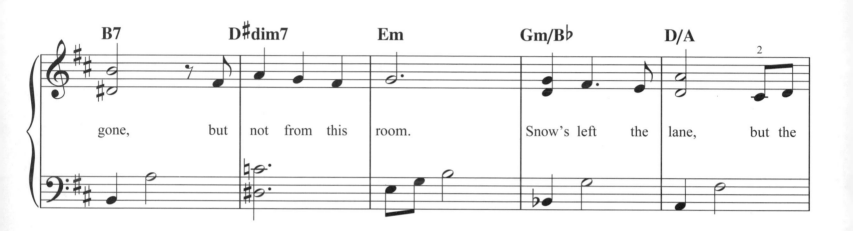

gone,   but not from this room.   Snow's left   the   lane,   but the

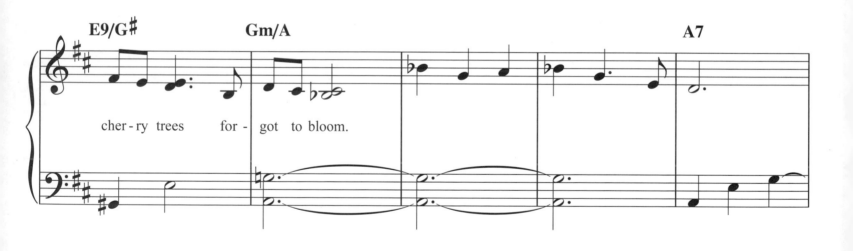

cher - ry trees   for - got to bloom.

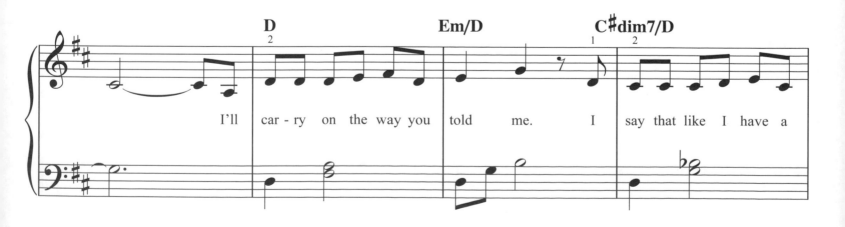

I'll   car - ry on the way you   told   me.   I   say that like I have a

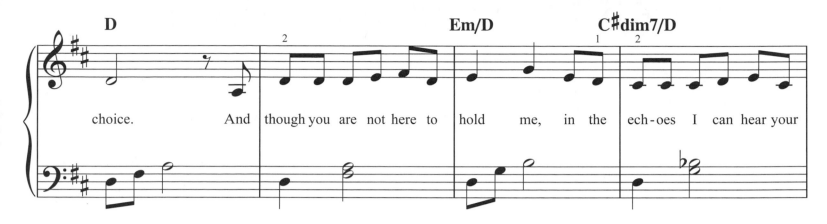

choice. And though you are not here to hold me, in the ech-oes I can hear your

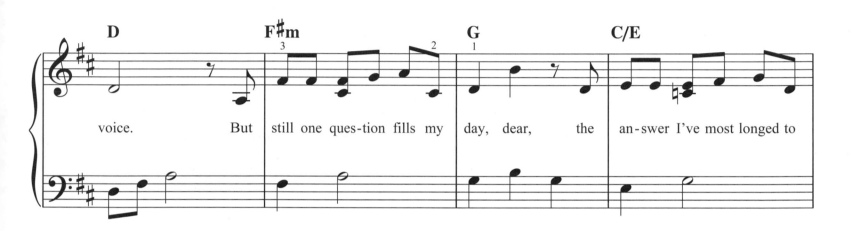

voice. But still one ques-tion fills my day, dear, the an-swer I've most longed to

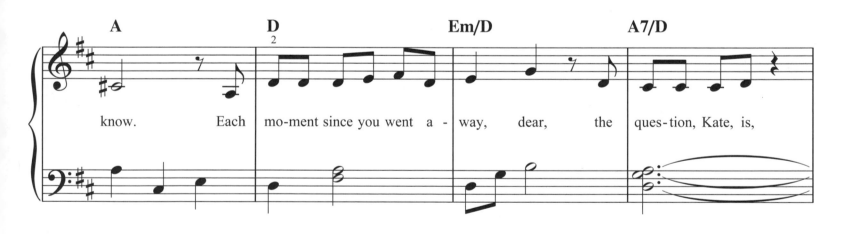

know. Each mo-ment since you went a - way, dear, the ques-tion, Kate, is,

(Spoken:) Where'd you go?

CAN YOU IMAGINE THAT?

Music by MARC SHAIMAN
Lyrics by SCOTT WITTMAN and MARC SHAIMAN

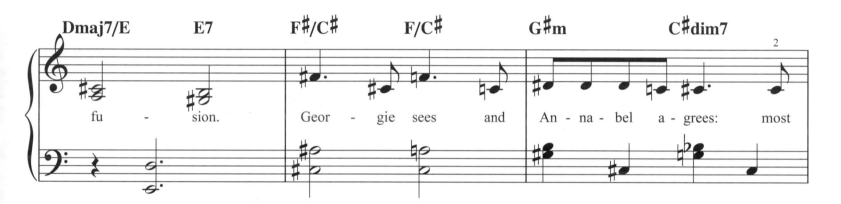

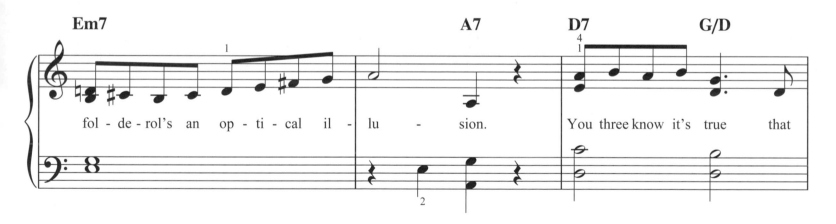

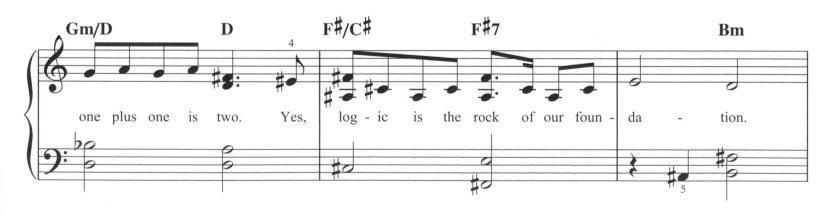

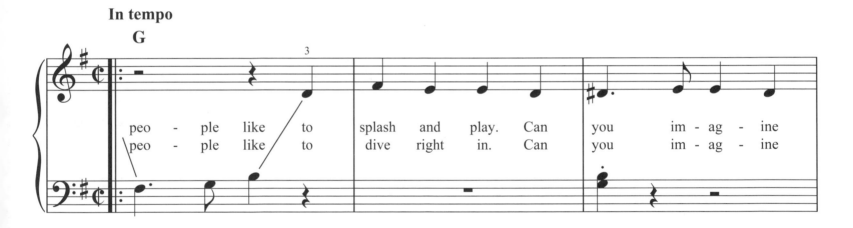

you im - ag - ine that? Too much glee leaves
you im - ag - ine that? Dog - gies pad - 'ling

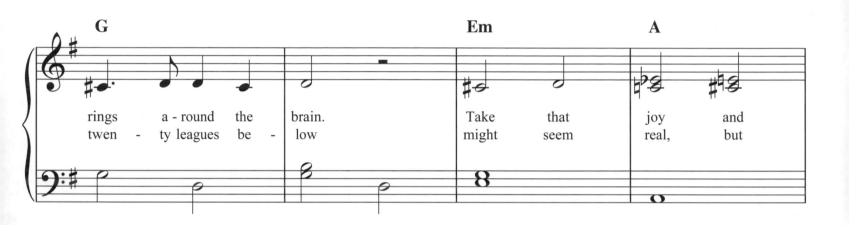

rings a - round the brain. Take that joy and
twen - ty leagues be - low might that seem real, but

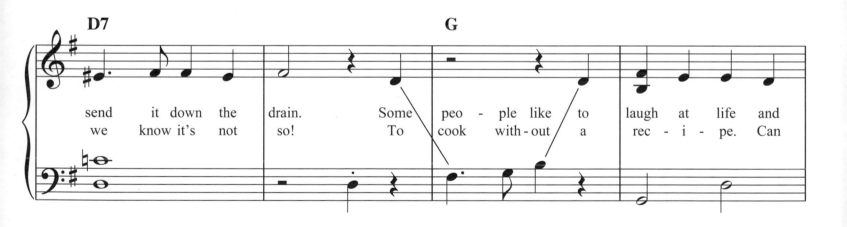

send it down the drain. Some peo - ple like to laugh at life and
we know it's not so! To cook with - out a rec - i - pe. Can

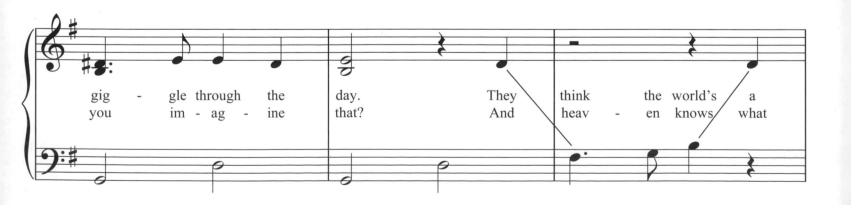

gig - gle through the day. They think the world's a
you im - ag - ine that? And heav - en knows what

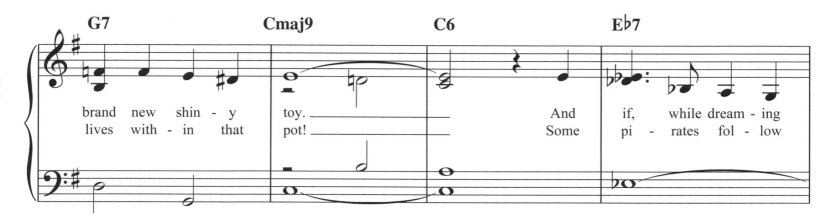

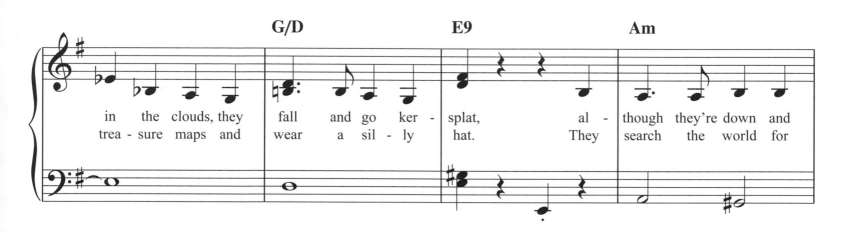

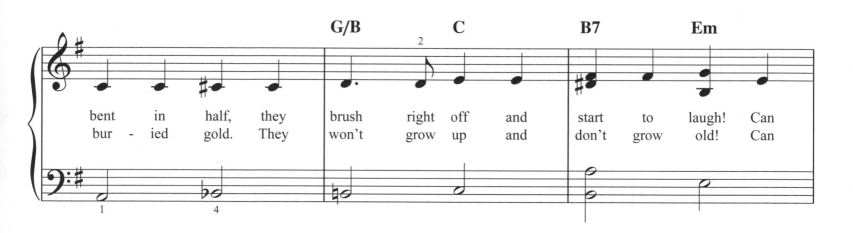

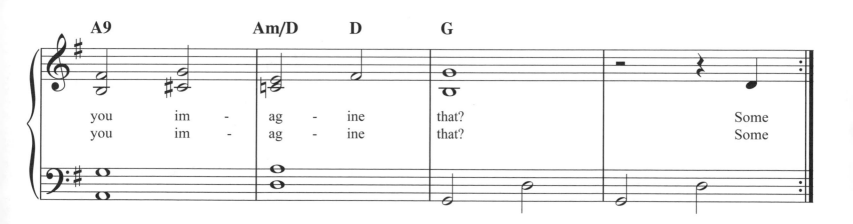

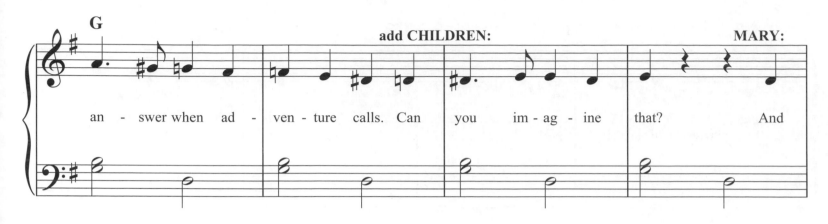

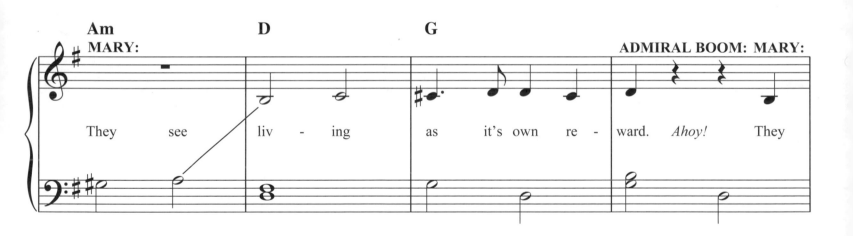

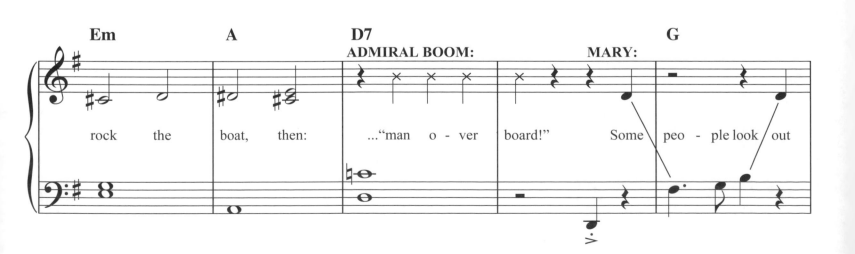

on the sea and   see a brand new   day.   Their   spir - it lifts them

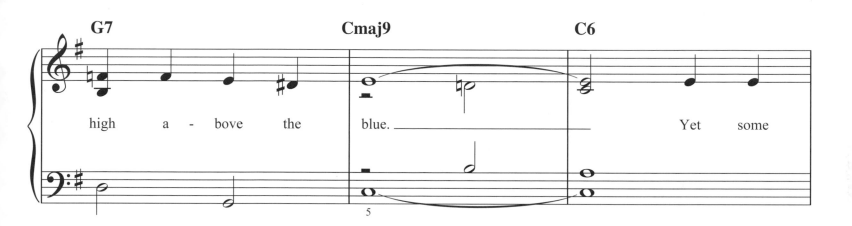

G7   **Cmaj9**   **C6**

high   a - bove the   blue. _____   Yet   some

Colla voce

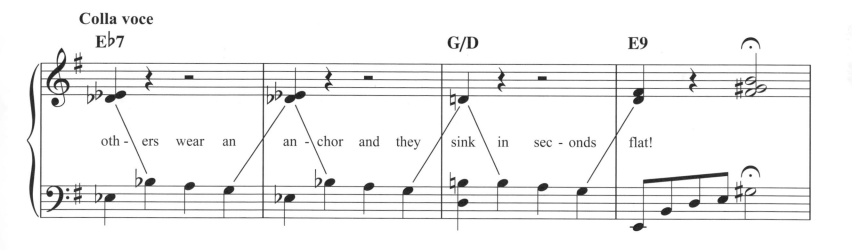

Eb7   **G/D**   **E9**

oth - ers wear an   an - chor and they   sink in sec - onds flat!

N.C.   **Am**   **G/B**   **C**

So,   per - haps we've learnt when   day   is done, some   stuff and non - sense

a tempo

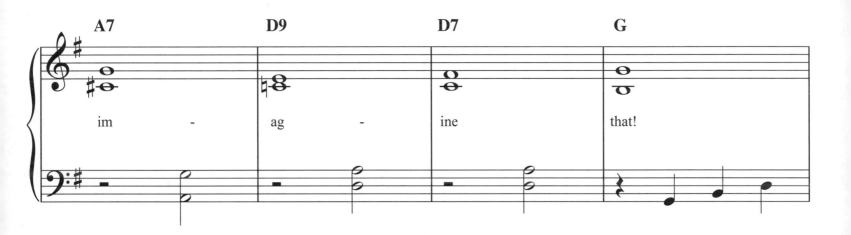

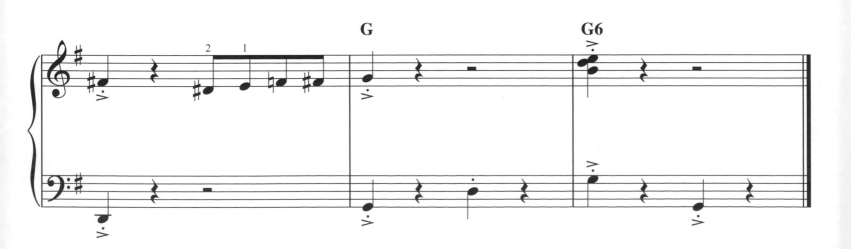

THE ROYAL DOULTON MUSIC HALL

Music by MARC SHAIMAN
Lyrics by SCOTT WITTMAN and MARC SHAIMAN

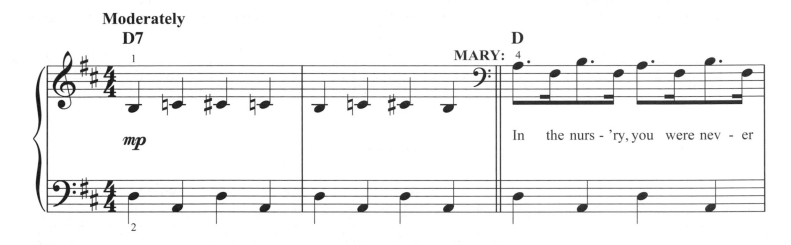

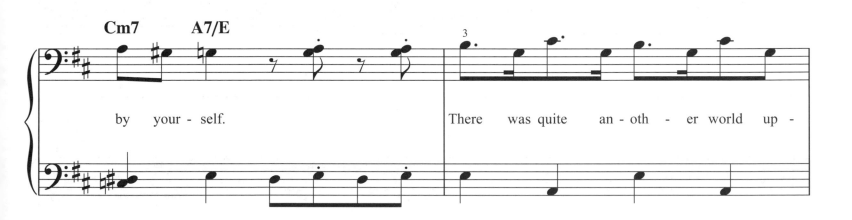

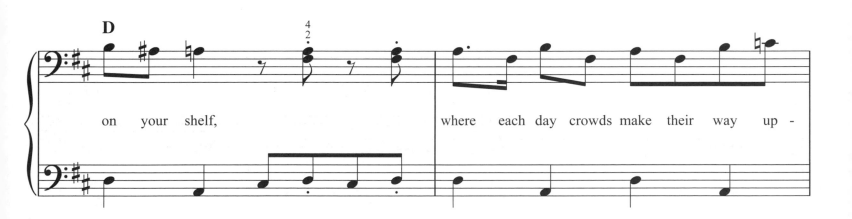

on the sun's de - scent to a myth - i - cal, mys - ti - cal, nev - er quite lo - gis - ti - cal

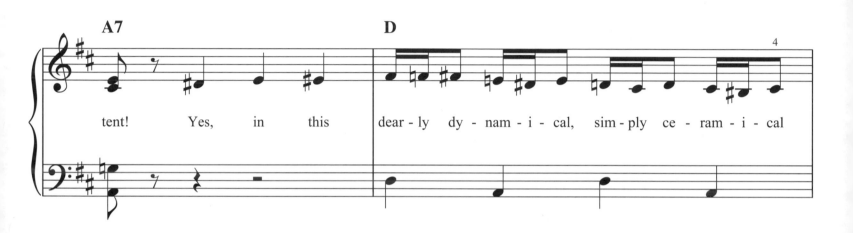

tent! Yes, in this dear - ly dy - nam - i - cal, sim - ply ce - ram - i - cal

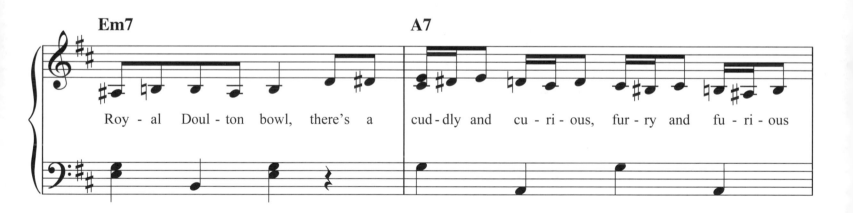

Roy - al Doul - ton bowl, there's a cud - dly and cu - ri - ous, fur - ry and fu - ri - ous

an - i - mal wat - 'ring hole, where the mon - keys and hum - ming - birds know the tunes and the words.

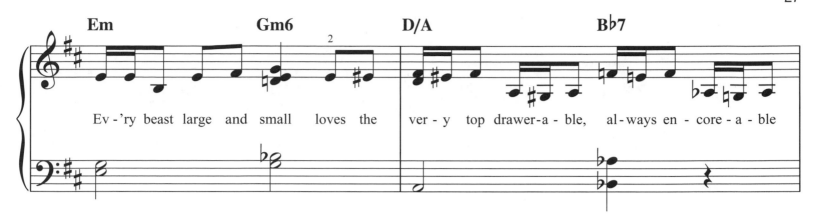

Ev -'ry beast large and small loves the ver - y top drawer-a - ble, al - ways en - core - a - ble

Roy - al Doul - ton Mu - sic Hall. Yes, in this

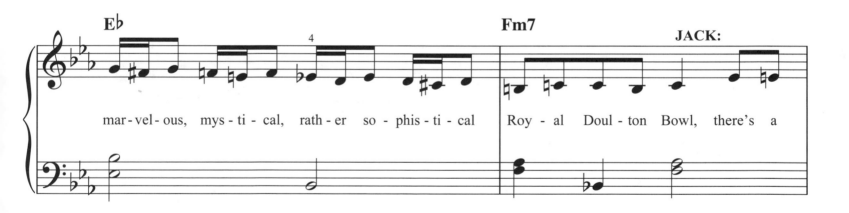

mar - vel - ous, mys - ti - cal, rath - er so - phis - ti - cal Roy - al Doul - ton Bowl, there's a

lot - ta birds queue-ing up, lot - ta hams chew-ing up scen - er - y they swal - low whole. There are

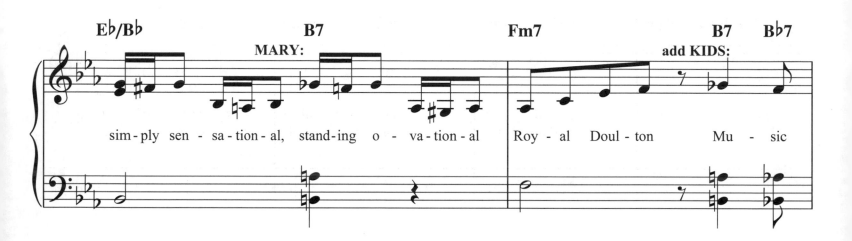

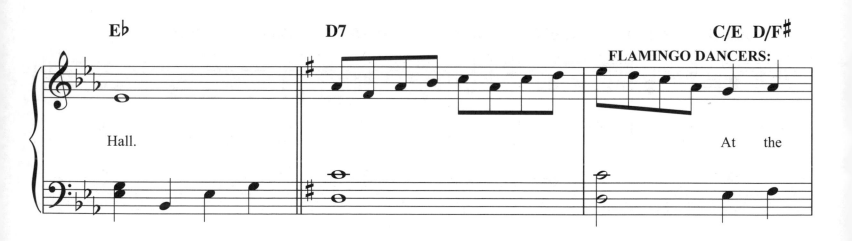

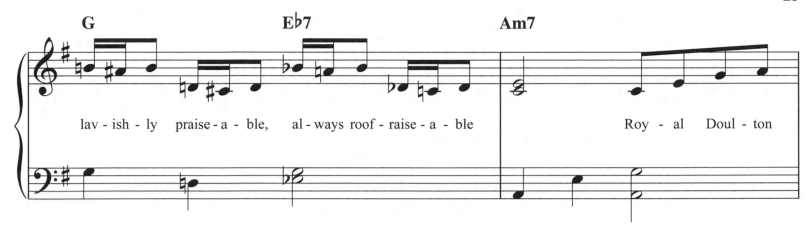

lav - ish - ly praise - a - ble, al - ways roof - raise - a - ble   Roy - al Doul - ton

Mu - sic Hall!

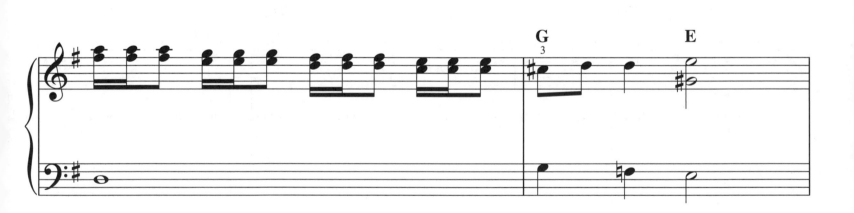

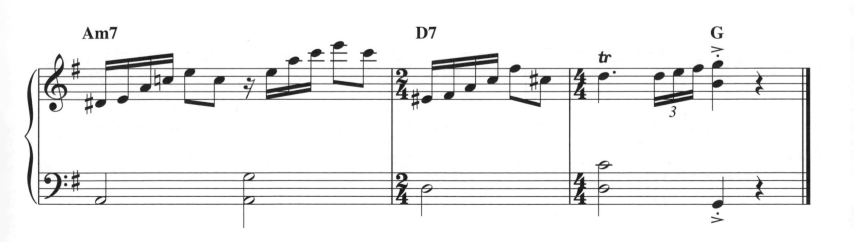

A COVER IS NOT THE BOOK

Music by MARC SHAIMAN
Lyrics by SCOTT WITTMAN and MARC SHAIMAN

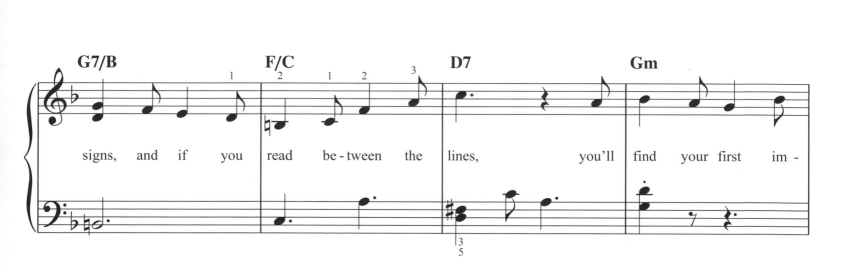

pres - sion was mis - took,   for a   cov - er is nice, but a

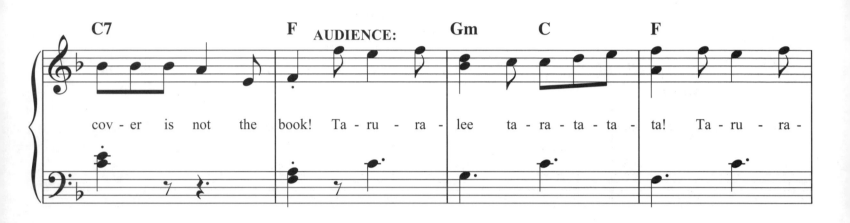

cov - er is not the   book! Ta - ru - ra - lee   ta - ra - ta - ta - ta! Ta - ru - ra -

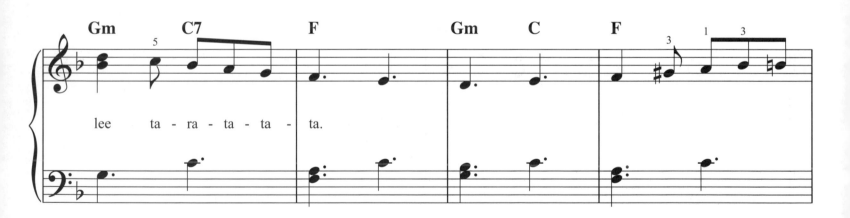

lee   ta - ra - ta - ta -   ta.

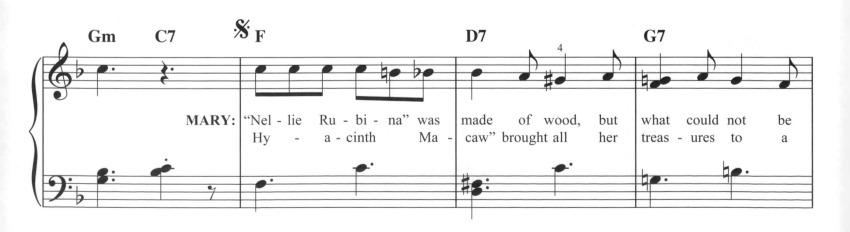

MARY: "Nel - lie Ru - bi - na" was   made   of wood, but   what could not be
       Hy - a - cinth Ma - caw" brought all   her   treas - ures to   a

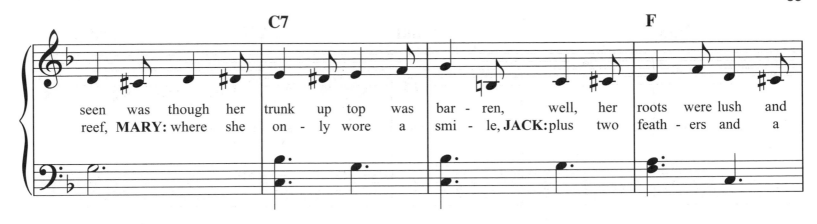

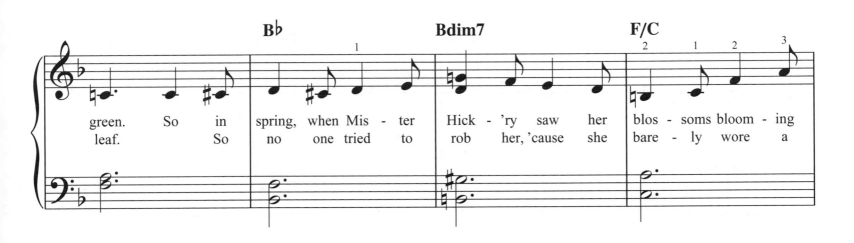

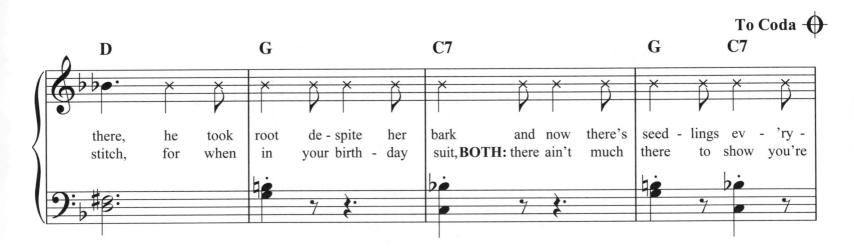

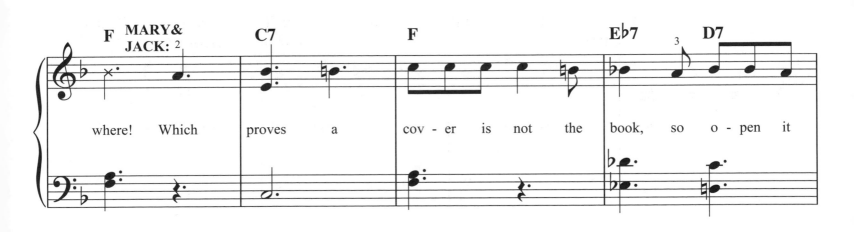

up and take a look, 'cause un-der the cov-ers, one dis-cov-ers that the

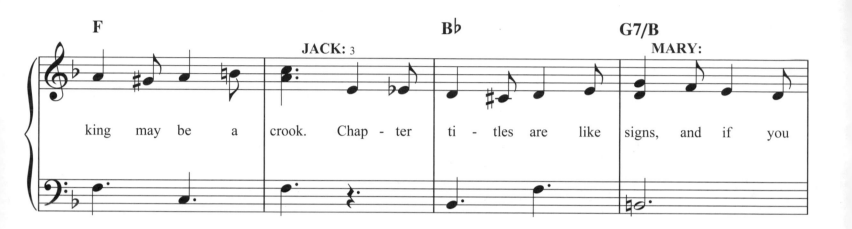

king may be a crook. Chap-ter ti-tles are like signs, and if you

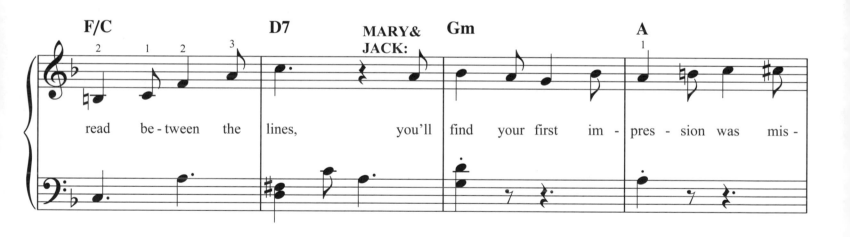

read be-tween the lines, you'll find your first im-pres-sion was mis-

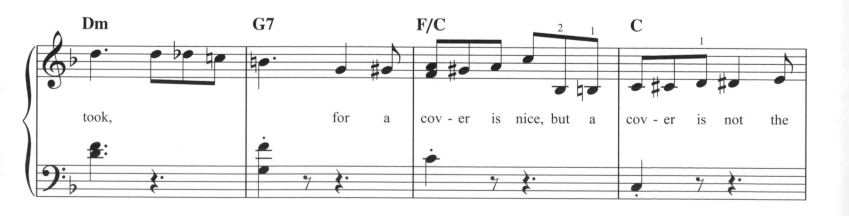

took, for a cov-er is nice, but a cov-er is not the

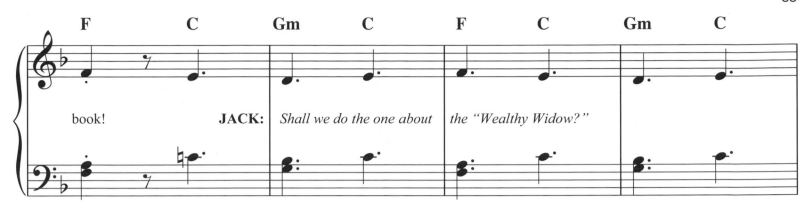

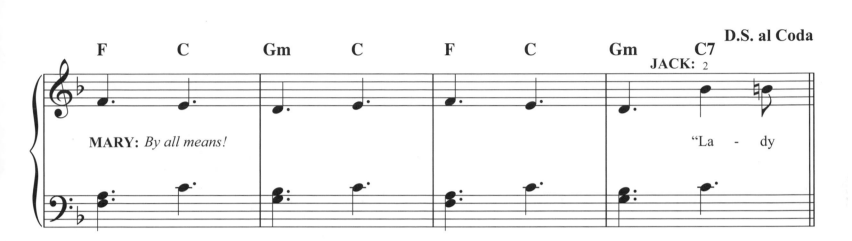

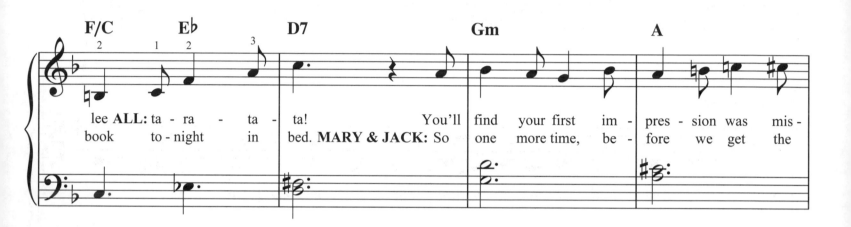

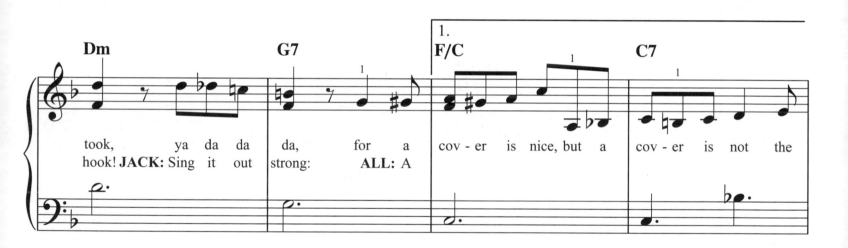

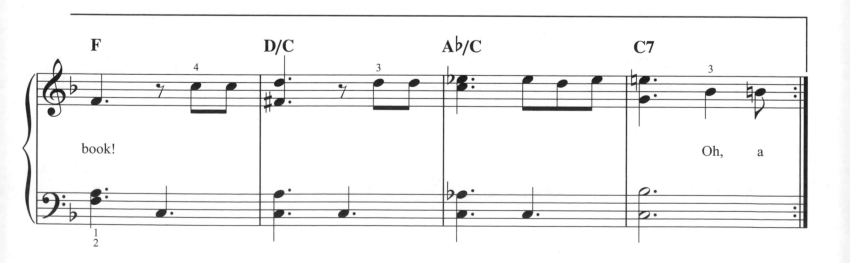

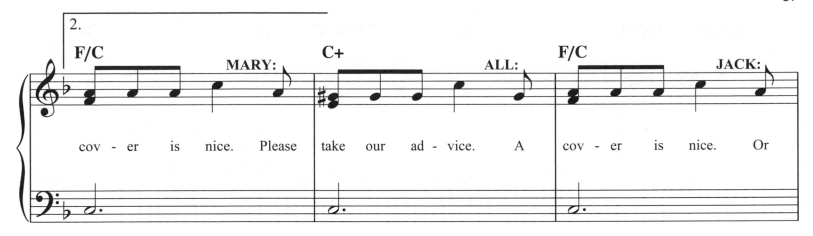

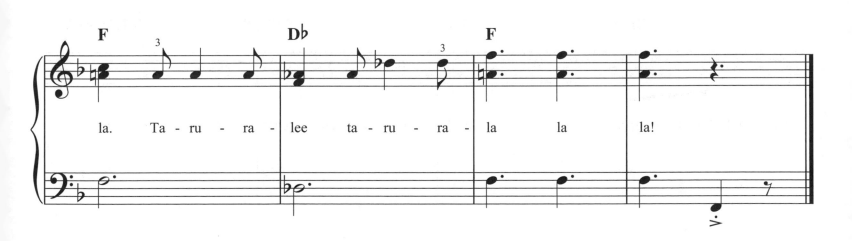

THE PLACE WHERE LOST THINGS GO

Music by MARC SHAIMAN
Lyrics by SCOTT WITTMAN and MARC SHAIMAN

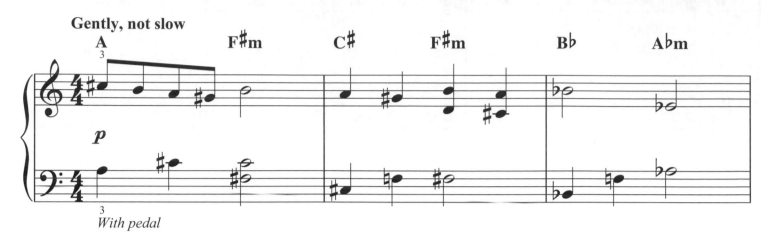

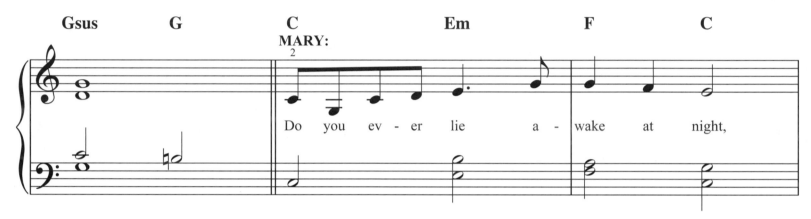

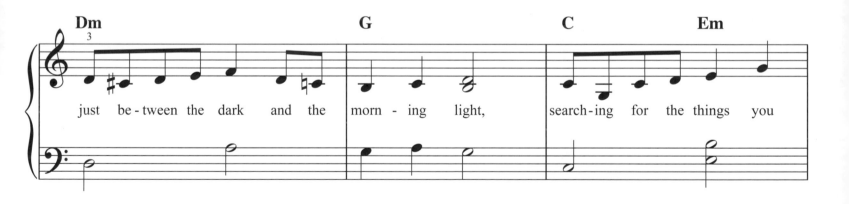

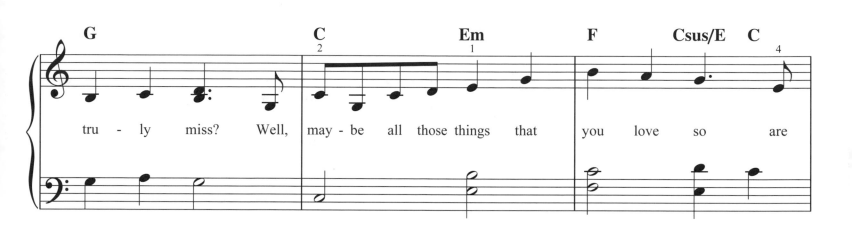

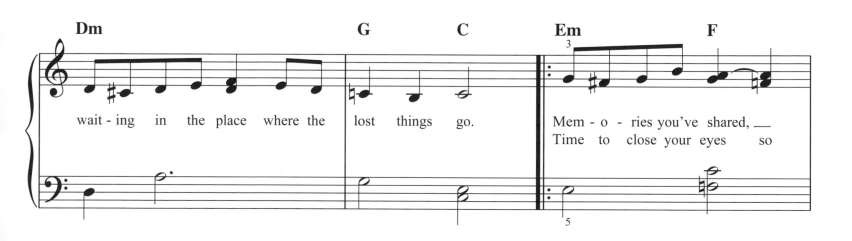

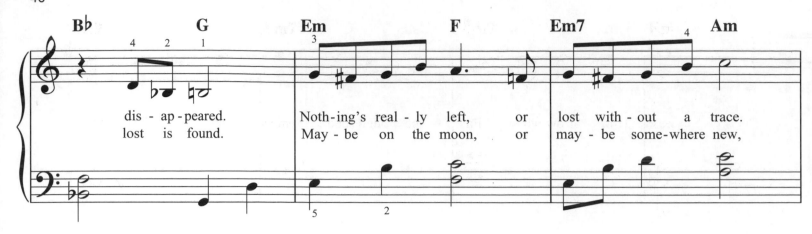

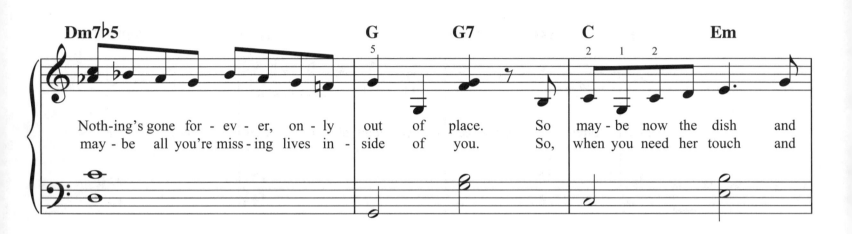

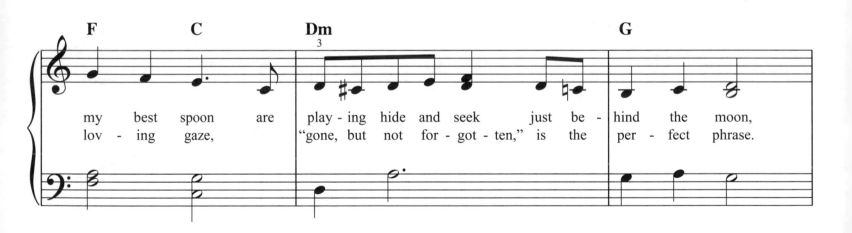

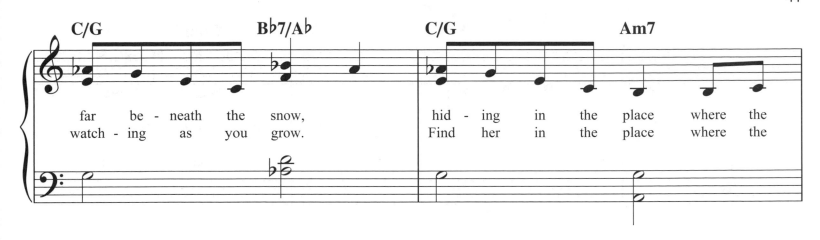

far be - neath the snow,
watch - ing as you grow.

hid - ing in the place where the
Find her in the place where the

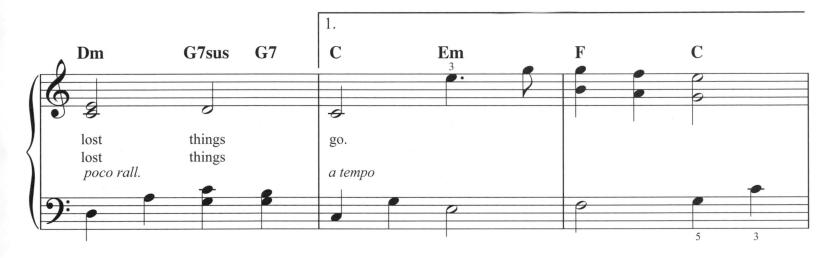

lost things
lost things
poco rall.

go.
a tempo

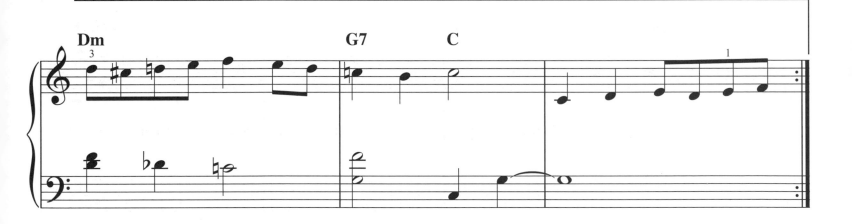

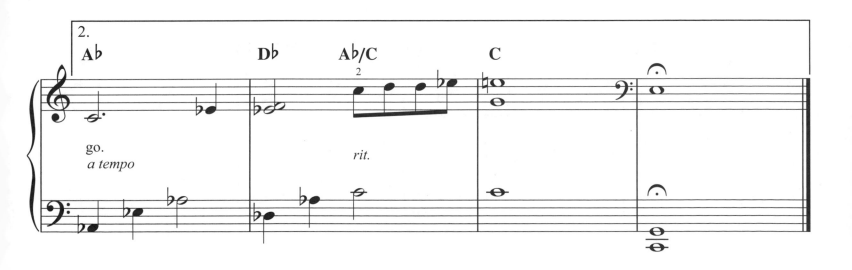

go.
a tempo

rit.

TURNING TURTLE

Music by MARC SHAIMAN
Lyrics by SCOTT WITTMAN and MARC SHAIMAN

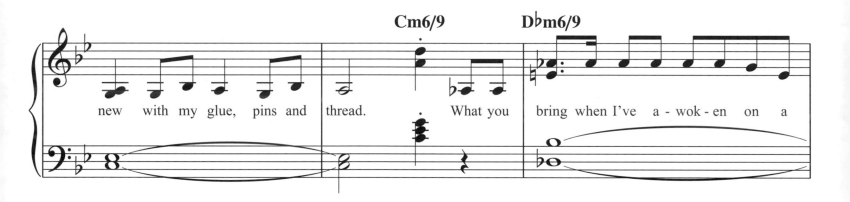

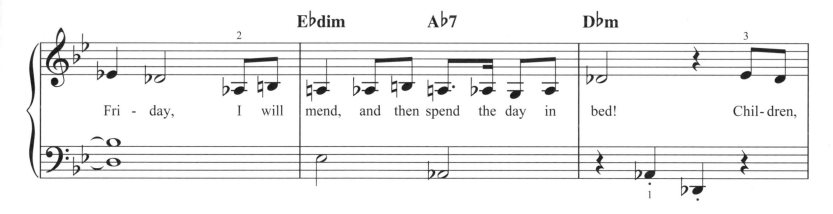

in the sec - ond week I wear a frown. For I

Moderately

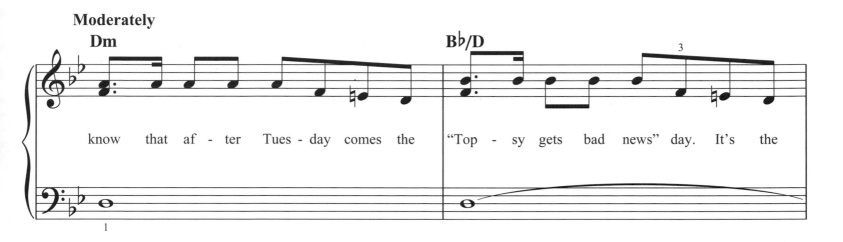

know that af - ter Tues - day comes the "Top - sy gets bad news" day. It's the

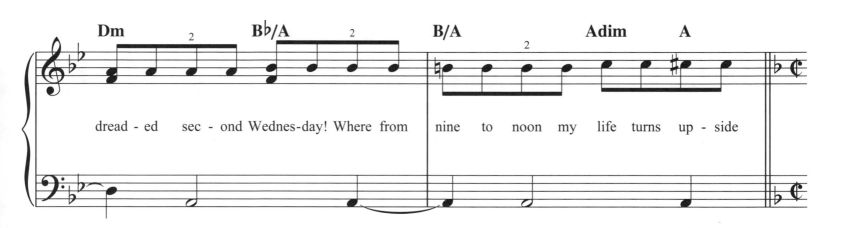

dread - ed sec - ond Wednes - day! Where from nine to noon my life turns up - side

Moderately fast, in 2

down! _____

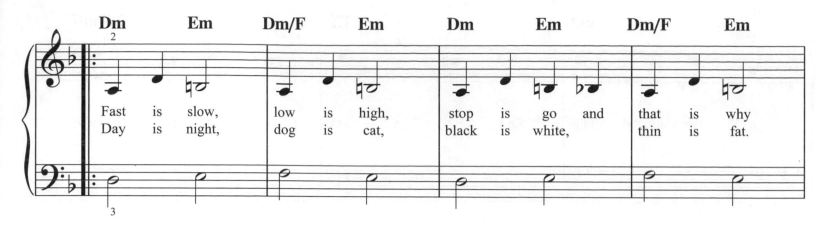

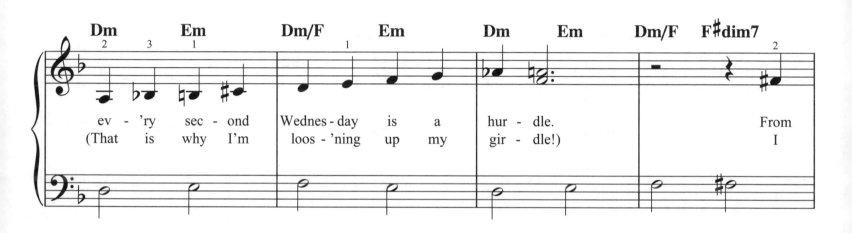

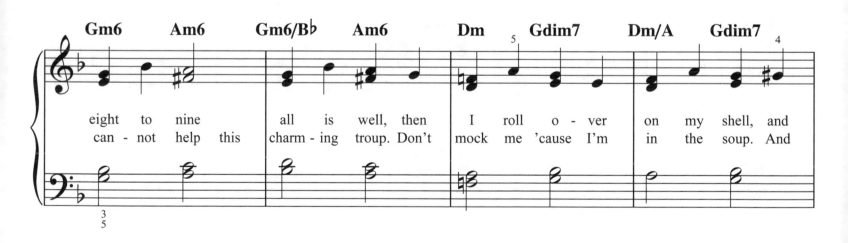

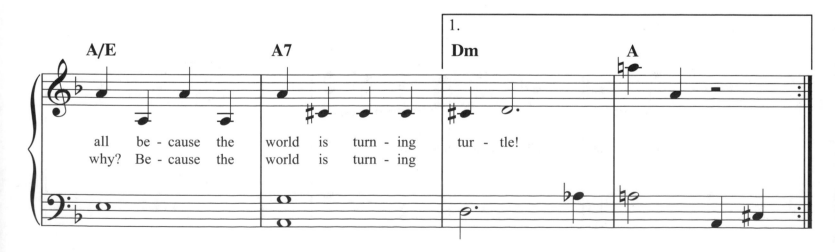

2.

Dm   Bb7   Dm/A

tur - tle!   Oh,   woe   is   me,   I'm   as   op - po-site   as

Bb7b5   A7   Dm   Edim7   Dm6/F   F#dim7

I   can   be!   I   long   for Thurs-days,   when   the world   is   drab.

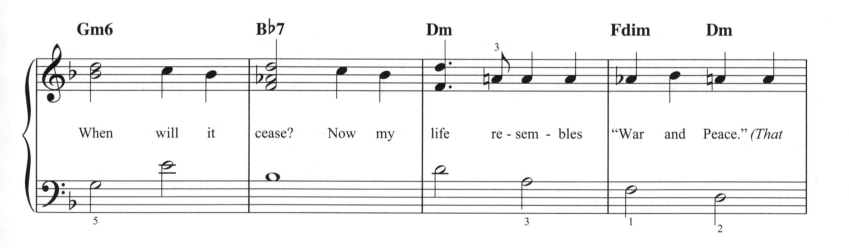

Gm6   Bb7   Dm   Fdim   Dm

When   will   it   cease?   Now   my   life   re - sem - bles   "War   and   Peace." *(That*

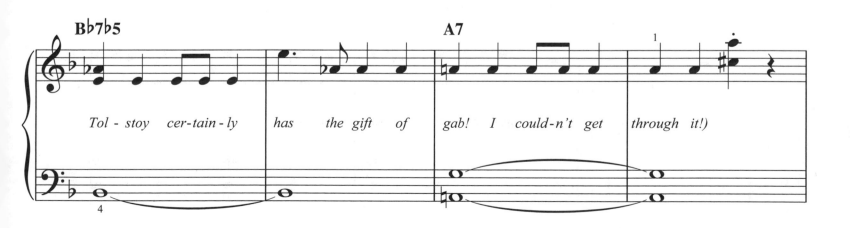

Bb7b5   A7

Tol - stoy   cer-tain-ly   has   the   gift   of   gab!   I   could-n't   get   through   it!)

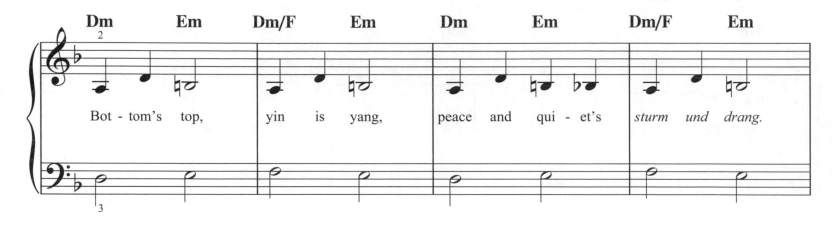

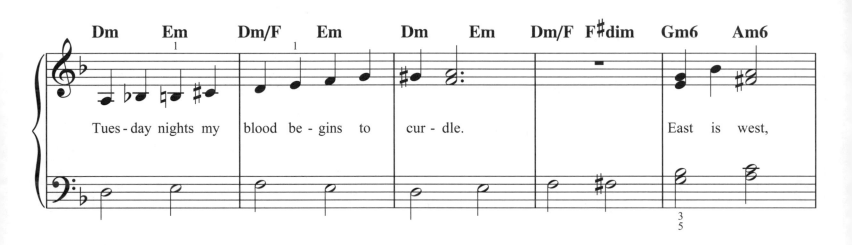

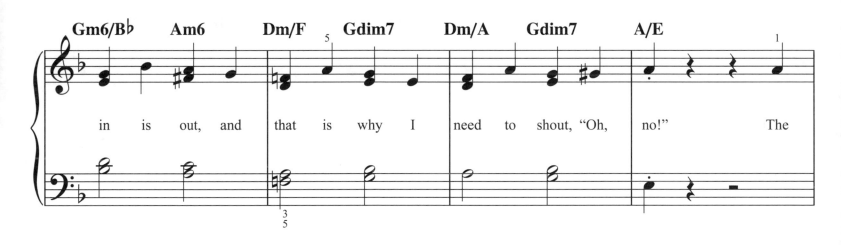

Oh, if   you   had   come   some   oth - er   morn, __   you
          could-n't mend this   to   save my   soul __   if

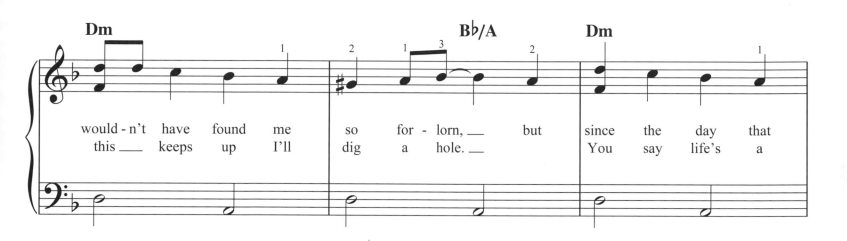

would - n't   have   found   me   so   for - lorn, __   but   since   the   day   that
this __   keeps   up   I'll   dig   a   hole. __   You   say   life's   a

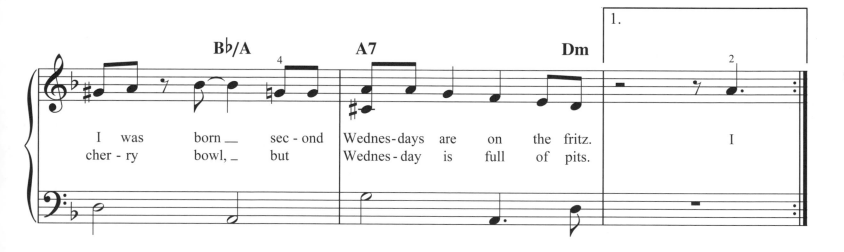

I   was   born __   sec - ond   Wednes-days are   on   the fritz.
cher - ry   bowl, __ but   Wednes-day is   full   of pits.   I

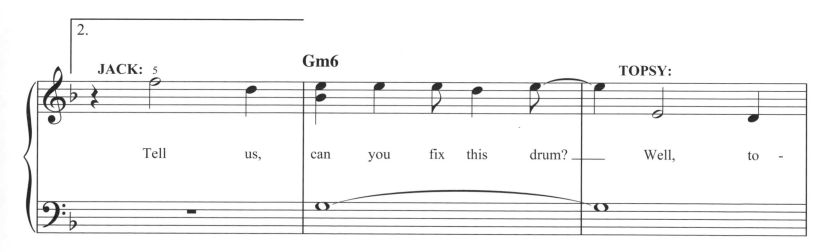

Tell   us,   can   you   fix   this   drum? __   Well,   to -

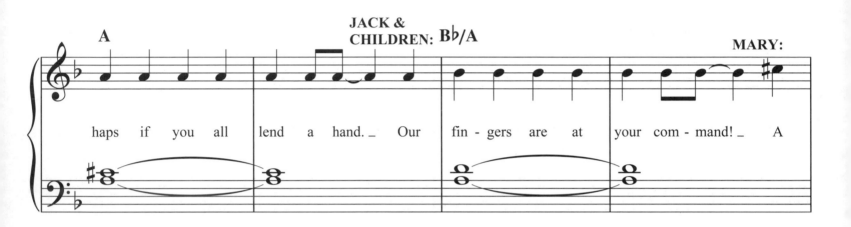

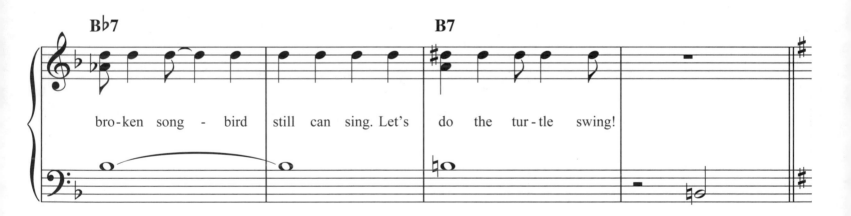

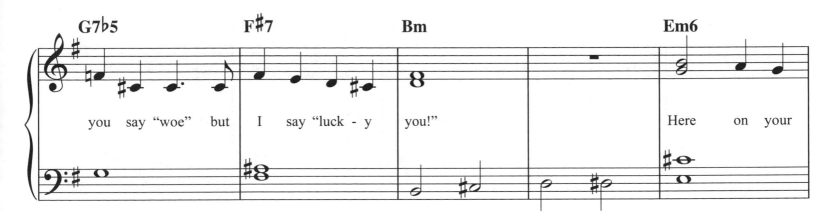

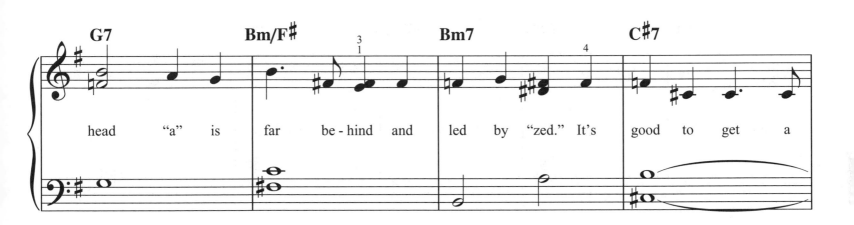

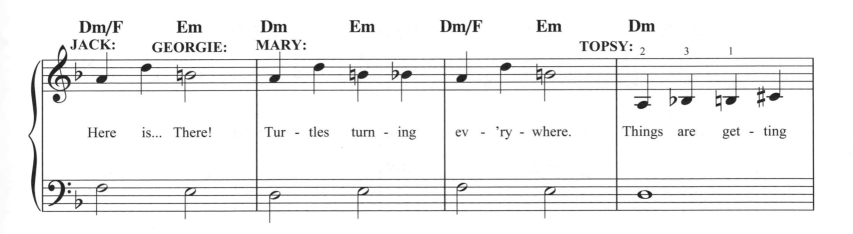

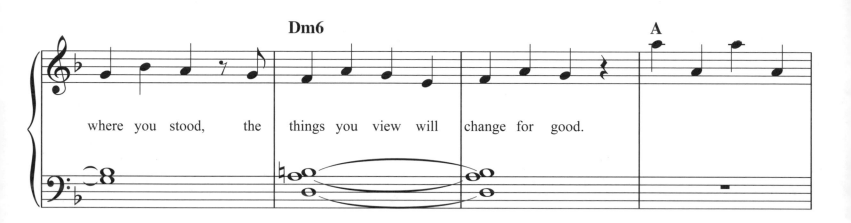

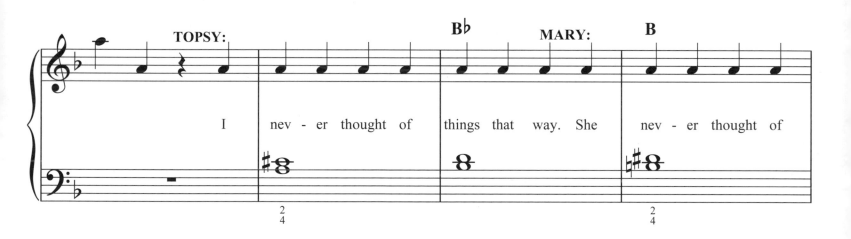

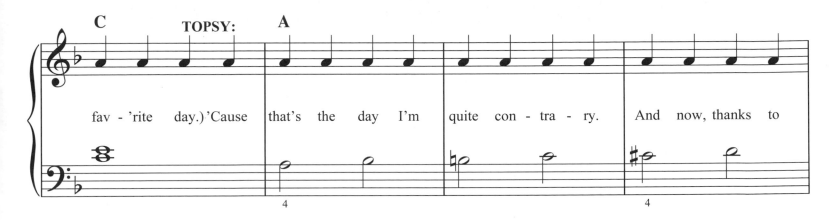

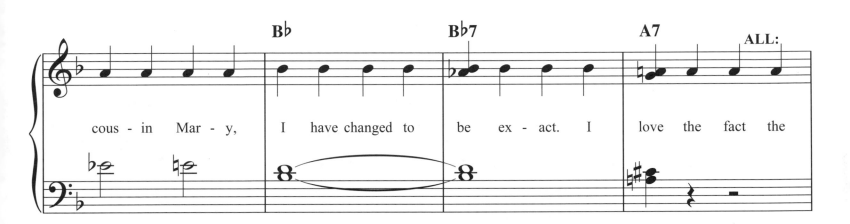

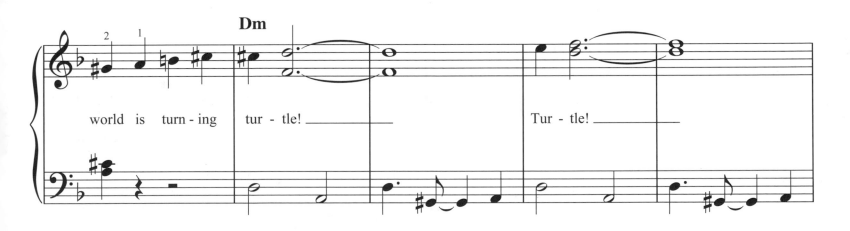

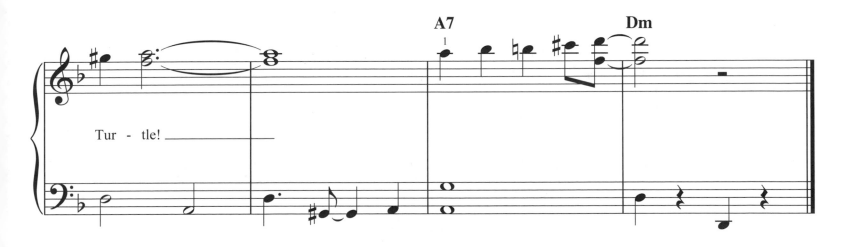

TRIP A LITTLE LIGHT FANTASTIC

Music by MARC SHAIMAN
Lyrics by SCOTT WITTMAN and MARC SHAIMAN

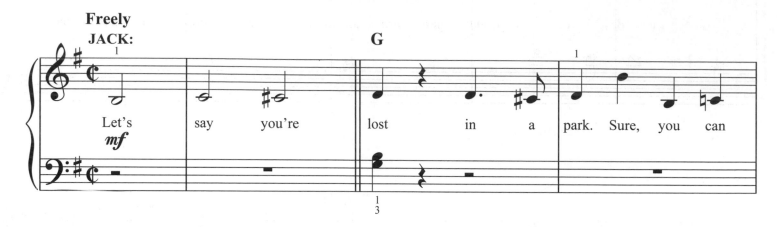

Let's say you're lost in a park. Sure, you can

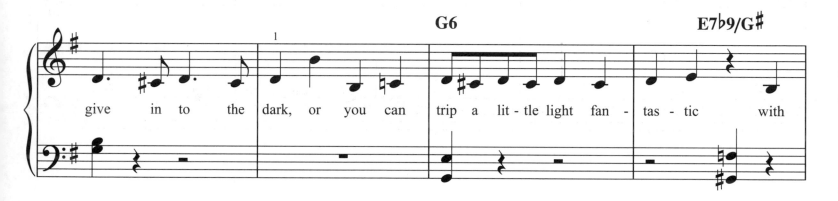

give in to the dark, or you can trip a lit-tle light fan - tas - tic with

me. When you're a - lone in your room, your choice is,

"Just em - brace the gloom," or you can trip a lit-tle light fan -

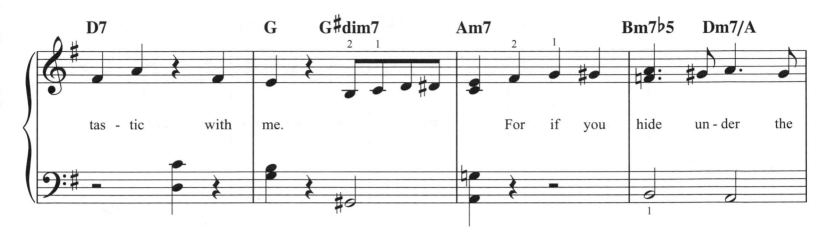

D7   **G**   **G♯dim7**   **Am7**   **Bm7♭5**   **Dm7/A**

tas - tic   with   me.   For   if   you   hide   un - der   the

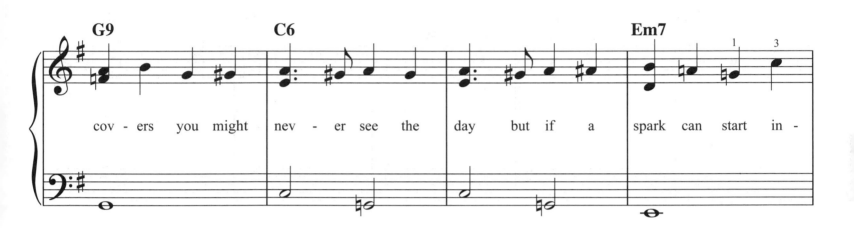

G9   **C6**   **Em7**

cov - ers   you   might   nev - er   see   the   day   but   if   a   spark   can   start   in -

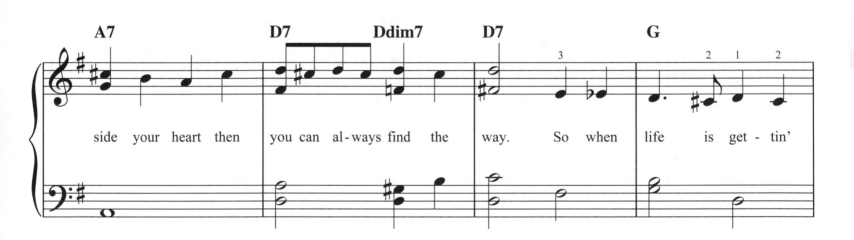

A7   **D7**   **Ddim7**   **D7**   **G**

side   your   heart   then   you   can   al - ways   find   the   way.   So   when   life   is   get - tin'

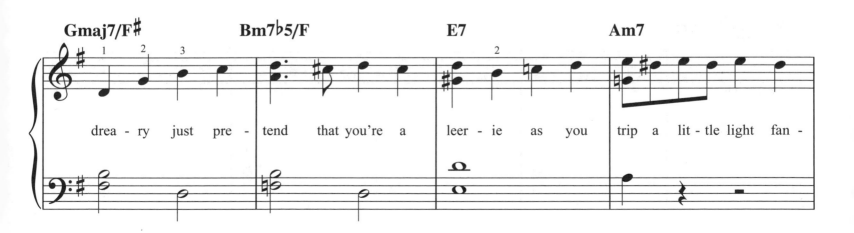

Gmaj7/F♯   **Bm7♭5/F**   **E7**   **Am7**

drea - ry   just   pre -   tend   that   you're   a   leer - ie   as   you   trip   a   lit - tle   light   fan -

54

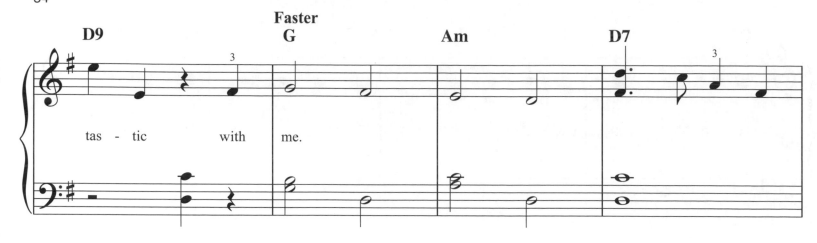

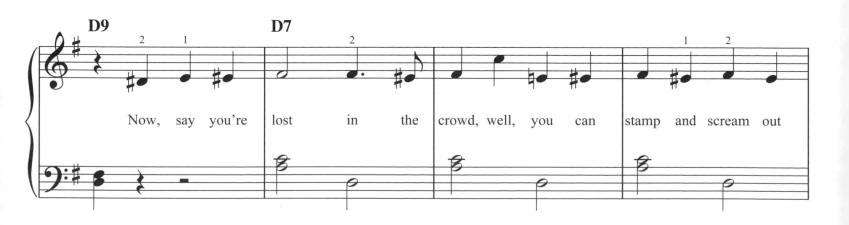

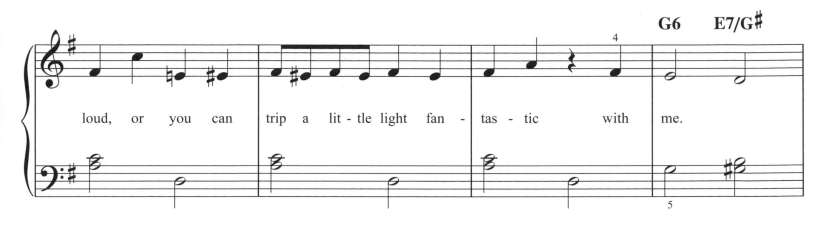

loud, or you can   trip a lit - tle light fan - tas - tic   with   me.

And when the   fog comes roll - ing   in just keep your   feet up - on the

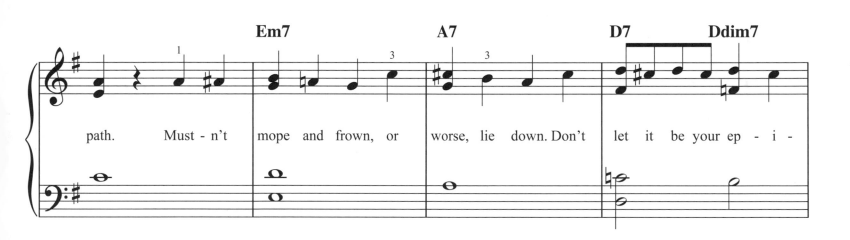

path.   Must - n't   mope and frown, or   worse, lie down. Don't   let it be your ep - i -

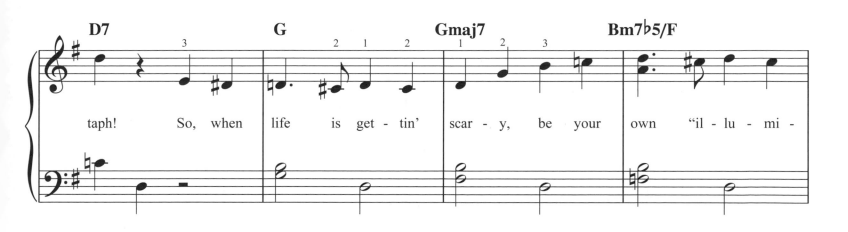

taph!   So, when   life is get - tin'   scar - y, be your   own "il - lu - mi -

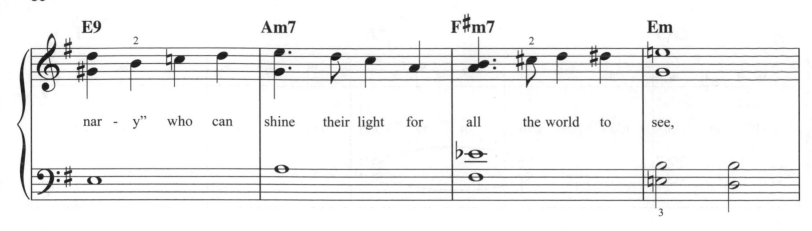

nar - y" who can shine their light for all the world to see,

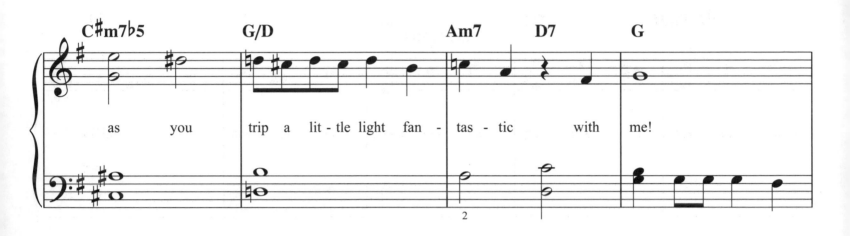

as you trip a lit - tle light fan - tas - tic with me!

Now if your life is get - tin' fog - gy, that's no

rea - son to com - plain. There's so much in store in - side the door of

Sev - en - teen Cher - ry Tree Lane.

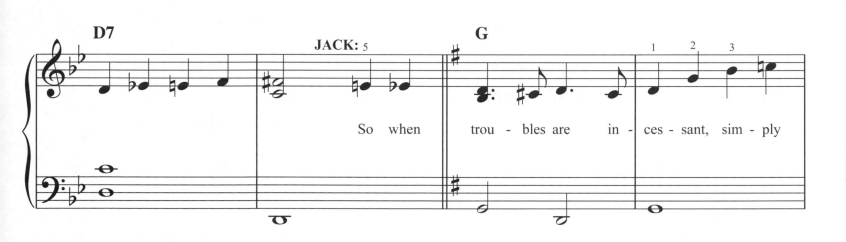

So when trou - bles are in - ces - sant, sim - ply

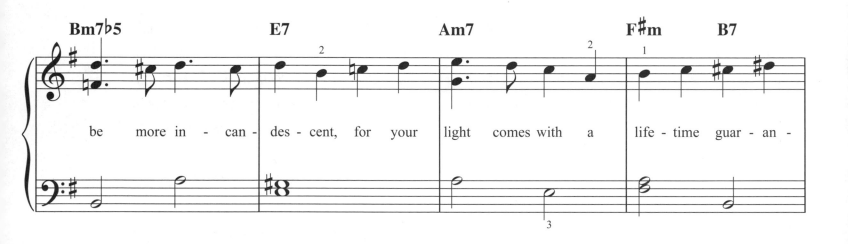

be more in - can - des - cent, for your light comes with a life - time guar - an -

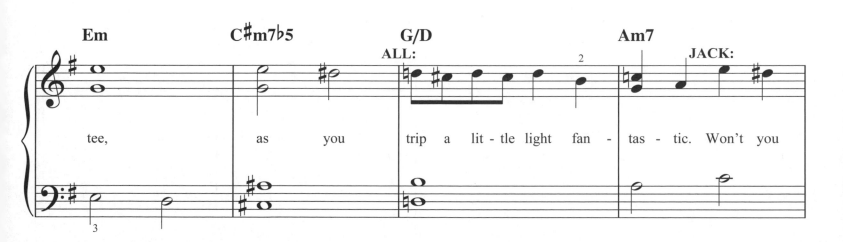

tee, as you trip a lit - tle light fan - tas - tic. Won't you

58

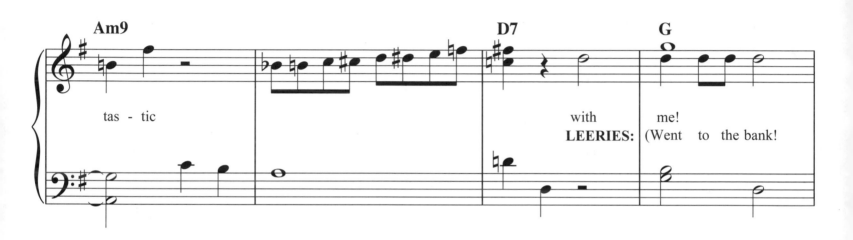

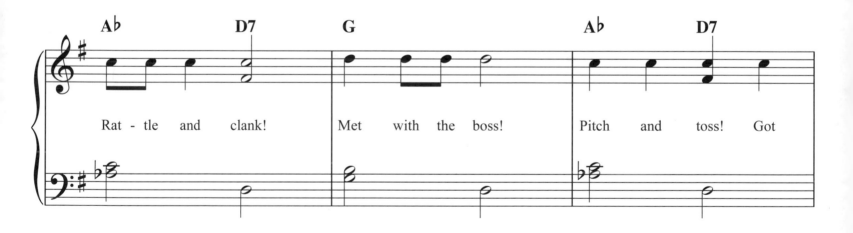

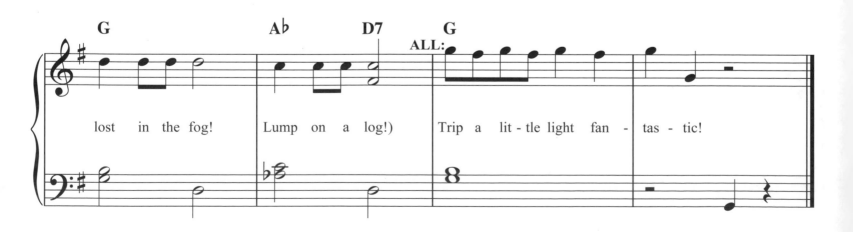

TRIP A LITTLE LIGHT FANTASTIC
(Reprise)

Music by MARC SHAIMAN
Lyrics by SCOTT WITTMAN and MARC SHAIMAN

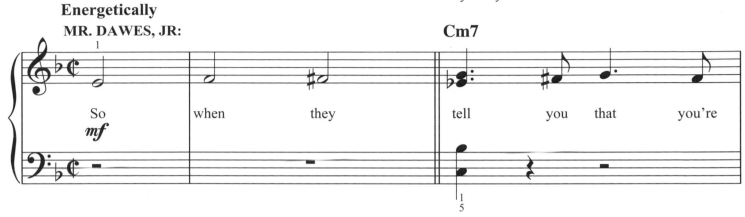

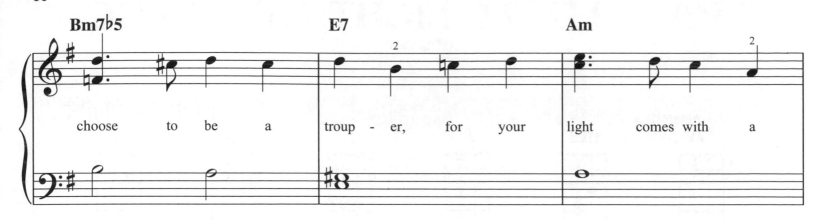

choose to be a troup - er, for your light comes with a

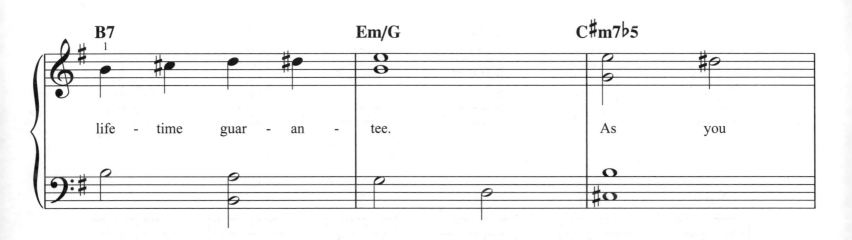

life - time guar - an - tee. As you

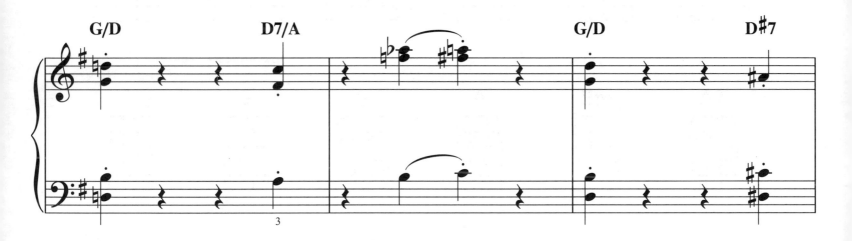

trip a lit - tle light fan - tas - tic

with me!
KIDS: (Went to the bank!

Rat - tle and clank! Met with the boss! Pitch and toss! Got

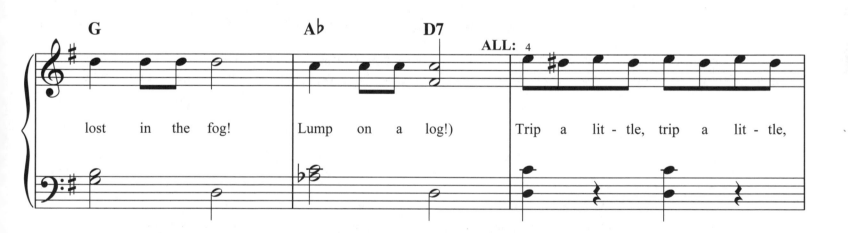

lost in the fog! Lump on a log!) Trip a lit - tle, trip a lit - tle,

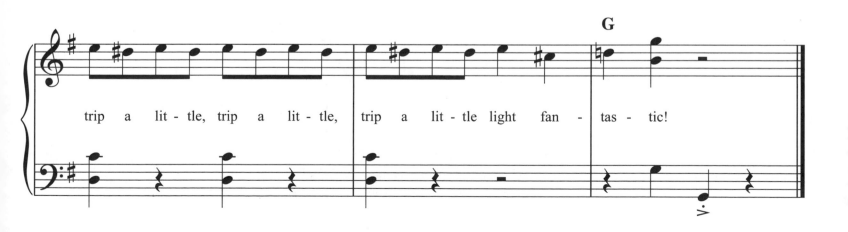

trip a lit - tle, trip a lit - tle, trip a lit - tle light fan - tas - tic!

NOWHERE TO GO BUT UP

Music by MARC SHAIMAN
Lyrics by SCOTT WITTMAN and MARC SHAIMAN

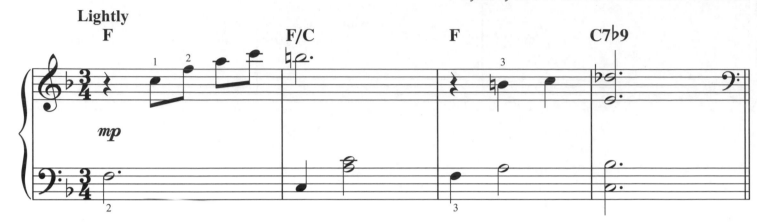

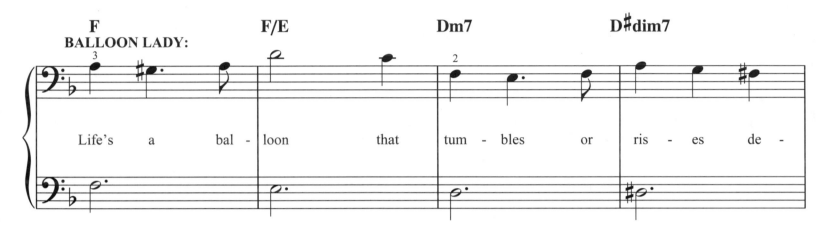

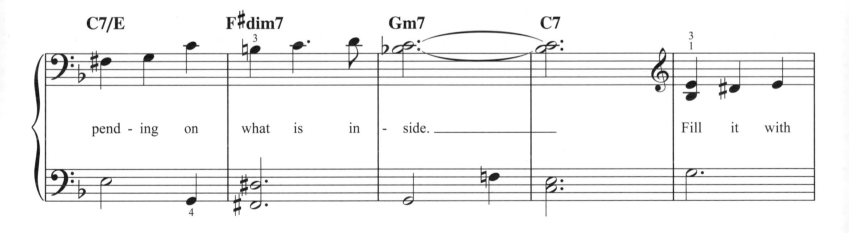

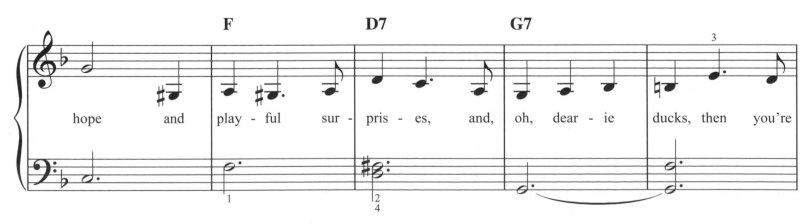

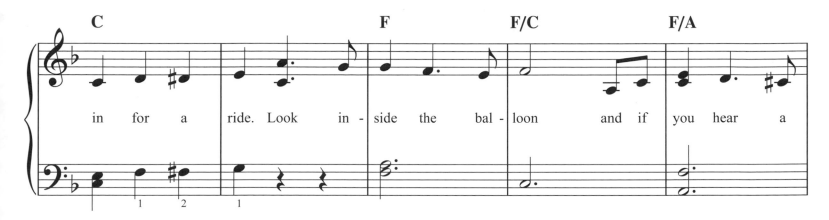

in for a ride. Look in-side the bal-loon and if you hear a

tune, there's no-where to go but up. Choose the

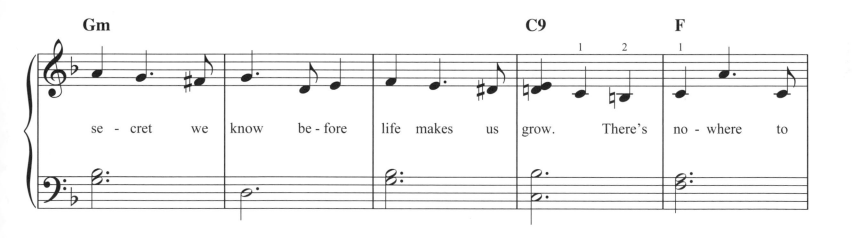

se-cret we know be-fore life makes us grow. There's no-where to

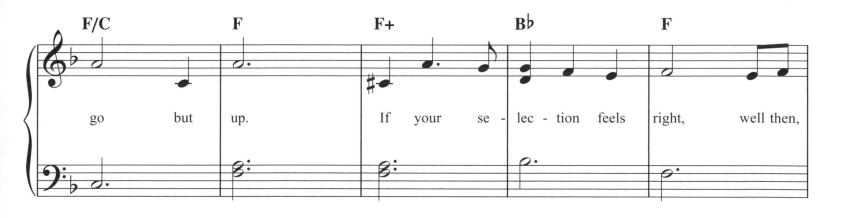

go but up. If your se-lec-tion feels right, well then,

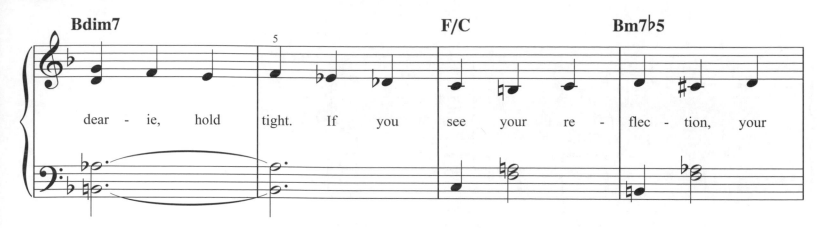

dear - ie, hold tight. If you see your re - flec - tion, your

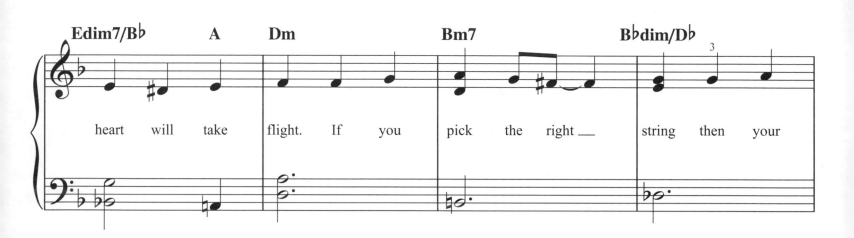

heart will take flight. If you pick the right __ string then your

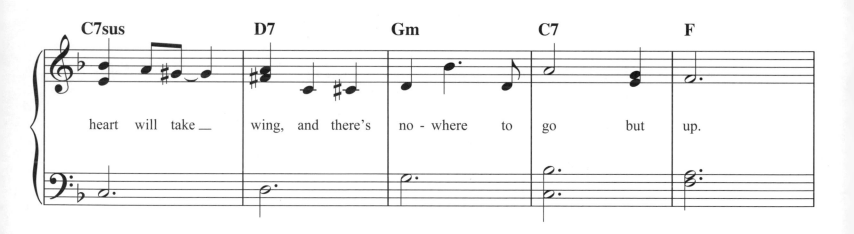

heart will take __ wing, and there's no - where to go but up.

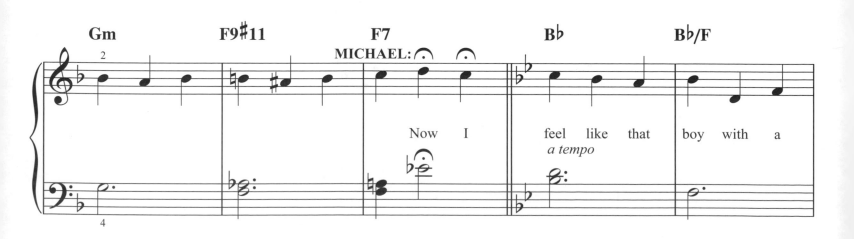

Now I feel like that boy with a

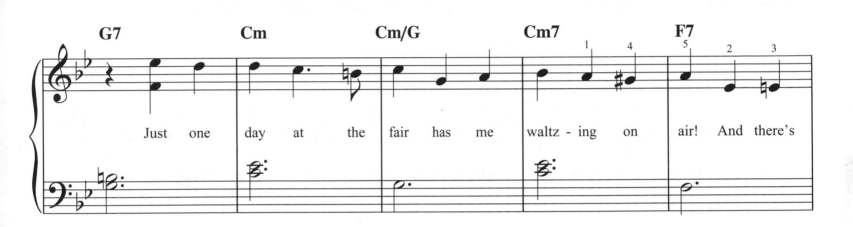

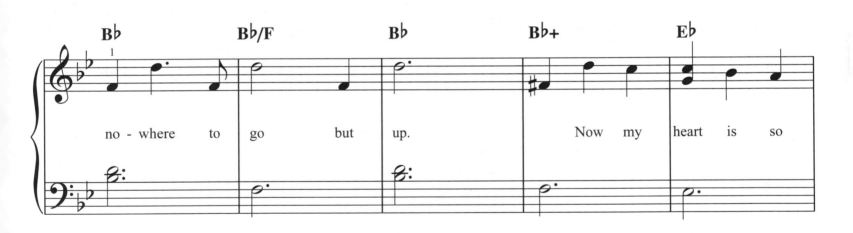

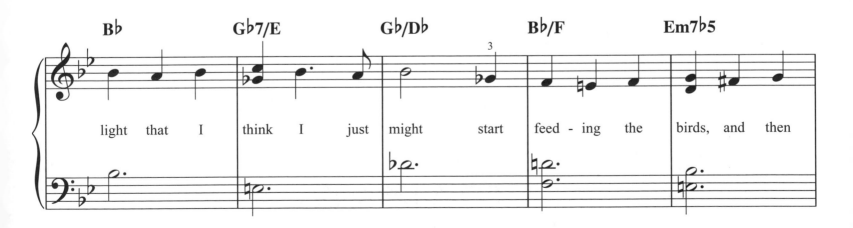

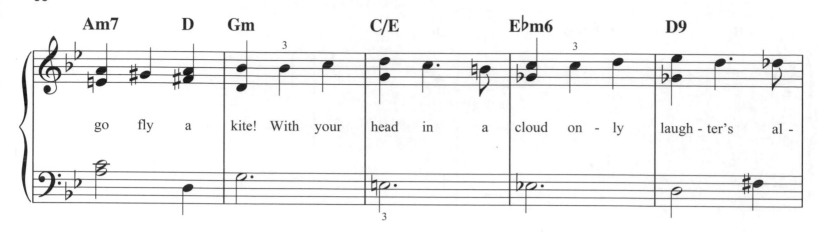

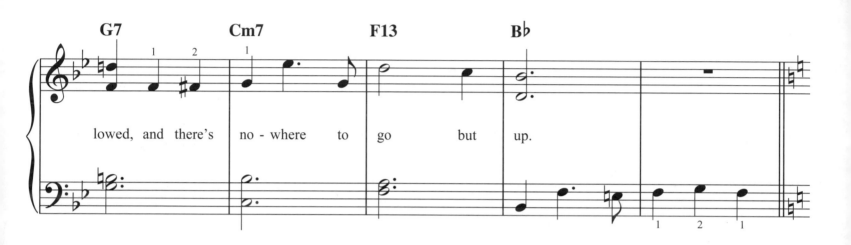

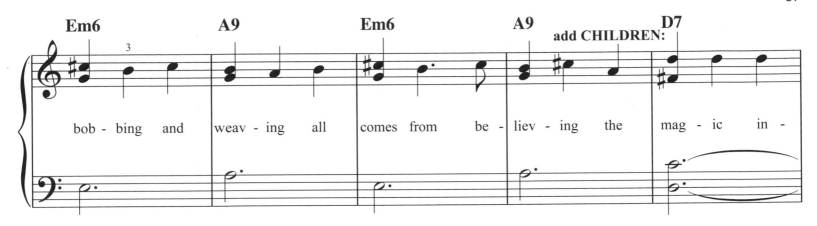

Em6   **A9**   **Em6**   **A9**   **add CHILDREN:**   **D7**

bob - bing and   weav - ing all   comes from   be - liev - ing the   mag - ic in -

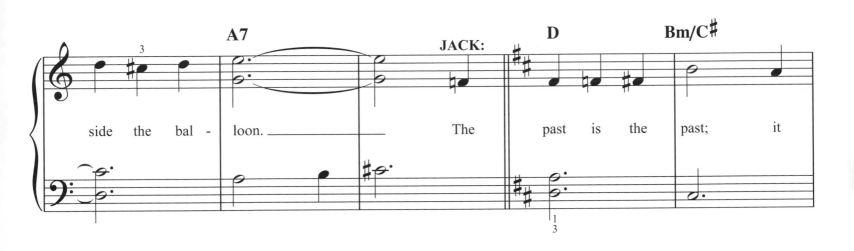

A7   **JACK:**   **D**   **Bm/C♯**

side the bal - loon. _____ The   past is the   past;   it

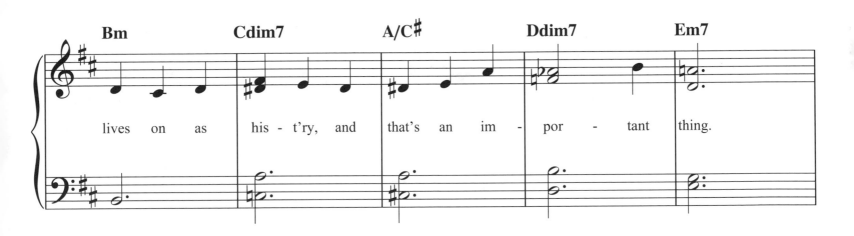

Bm   **Cdim7**   **A/C♯**   **Ddim7**   **Em7**

lives on as   his - t'ry, and   that's an im -   por - tant   thing.

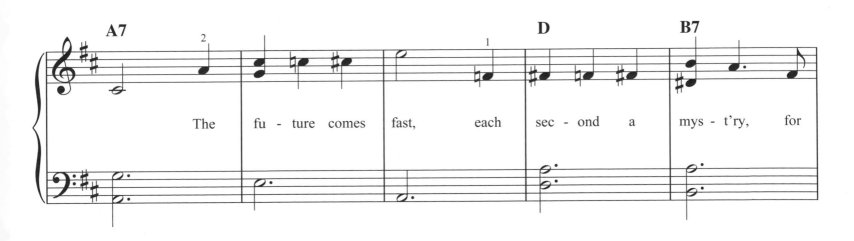

A7   **D**   **B7**

The   fu - ture comes   fast,   each   sec - ond a   mys - t'ry, for

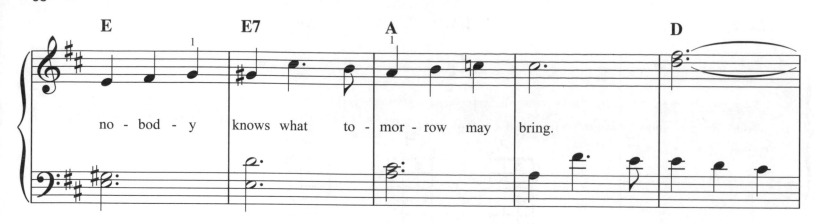

no - bod - y   knows what   to - mor - row may   bring.

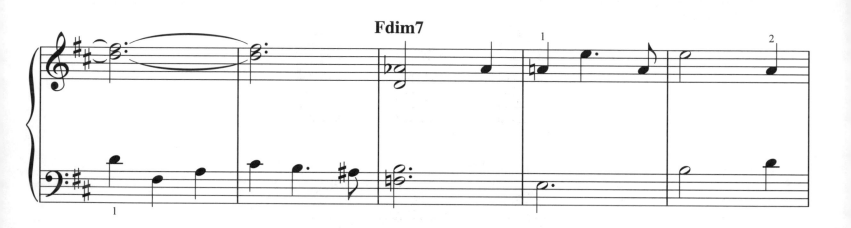

Up   here   in   the   blue it's a   mar - vel - ous

view! Side by   side   is   the   best way   to   fly.   Once I

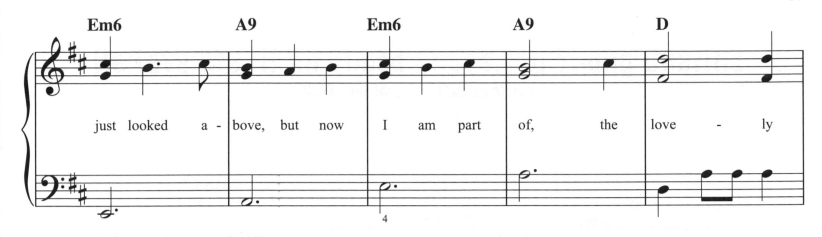

just looked a - bove, but now I am part of, the love - ly

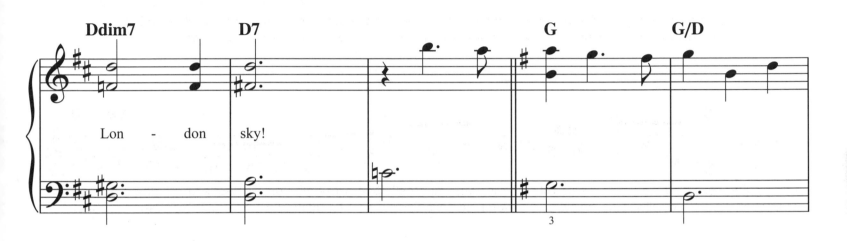

Lon - don sky!

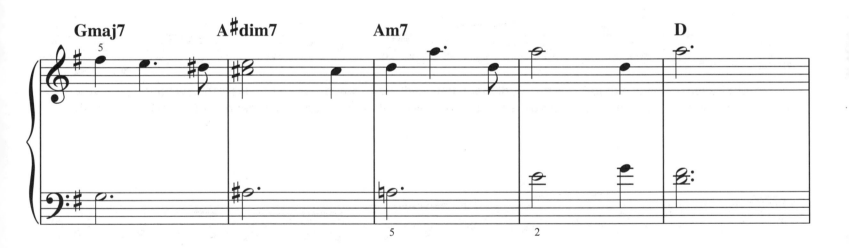

Well, there's

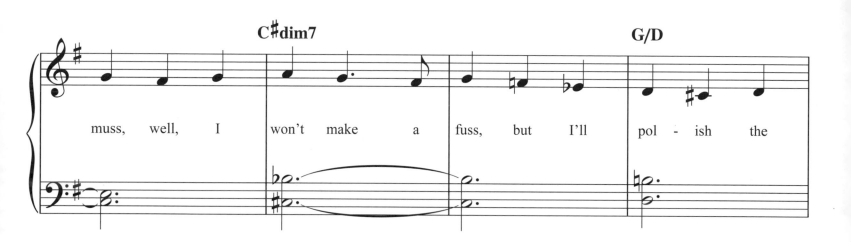

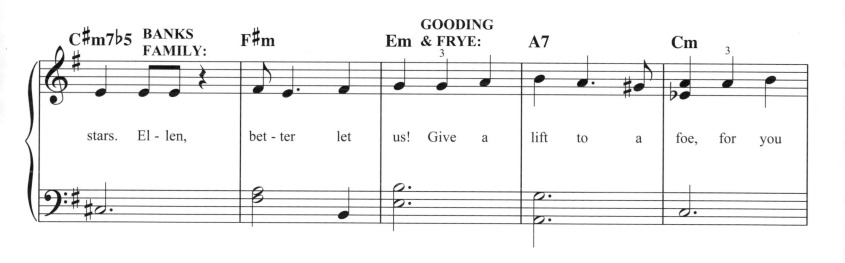

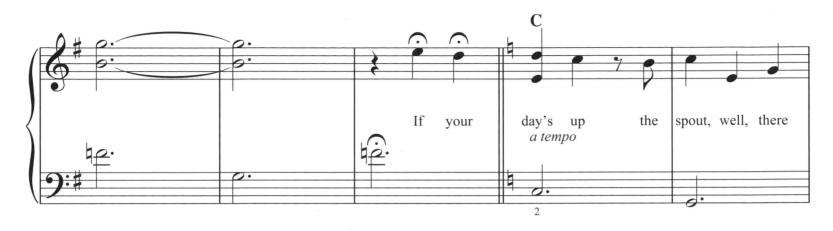

a tempo

If your day's up the spout, well, there

D♯dim7　　　**Dm11**　　　　　　　　　**G**

is - n't a doubt there's no - where to go but up.

A7　　　**Dm**

And if you don't be - lieve, just hang on to my

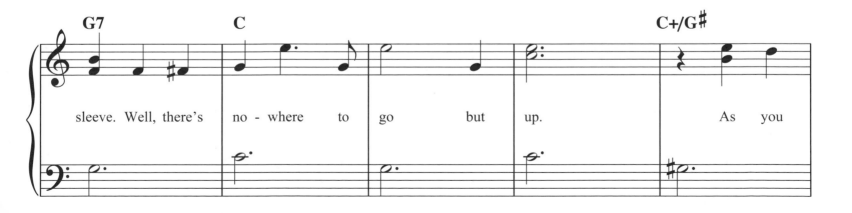

G7　　　**C**　　　　　　　　　　　　　**C+/G♯**

sleeve. Well, there's no - where to go but up.　As you

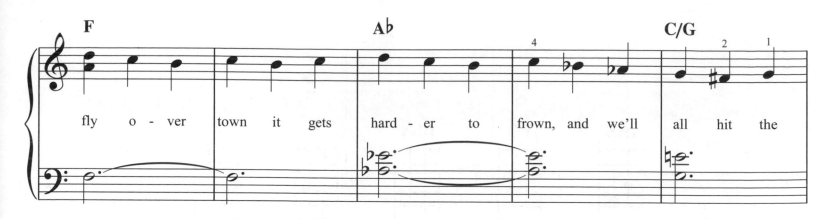

fly o - ver town it gets hard - er to frown, and we'll all hit the

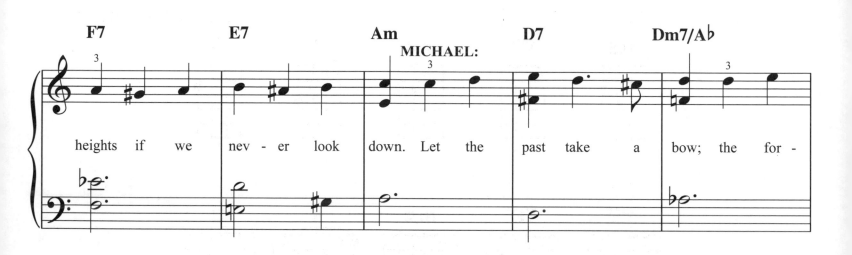

heights if we nev - er look down. Let the past take a bow; the for -

ev - er is now. And there's no - where to go but up,

up! There's no - where to go but up!